The Mosaic of My Life

To order additional copies of this book, contact:
Xlibris
844-714-8691
www.Xlibris.com
Orders@Xlibris.com

ISBN: Softcover   978-1-6641-2875-0
        Hardcover   978-1-6641-2876-7
        EBook   978-1-6641-2874-3

Print information available on the last page

Rev. date: 09/23/2020

The Mosaic of My Life

Hosain Mosavat

Credits

I, Hosain's wife, Judy, have a number of people to thank for contributing beautifully to the making of Hosain Mosavat's autobiography. First and foremost, are Ginger Wiechers and Babak Rowshan for sitting down with Hosain and me one evening every two weeks for quite some time. They brought a meal and then afterwards, we asked Hosain questions about his extraordinary life and recorded his answers. We brought in friends and family by email to offer questions for him, as well. This is what made this book possible and I'm deeply grateful for everyone's participation.

The front cover was created by Rosie Lemons. She took Hosain's photographs and designed a beautiful mosaic of his extraordinary photographic talent. Rosie also contributed by working on some of the photographs in this book to convert them to Black & White.

I, Judy Mosavat, took the photograph of Hosain on the back cover. The poem is by Hosain.

Chapter 1: Drawing by Howard Weingarden.

Chapter 2: These photographs of Hosain's parents are decades old and were taken by someone in Iran. They were adjusted by John Lloyd.

Chapter 3: The photograph of Hosain and his son, David, was taken by Judy Mosavat.

Chapter 4: The first musical instrument, the dombak, was photographed by Judy Mosavat. The sitar, santur and dafs and steel drums were photographed by John Lloyd.

Chapter 6: The grill was photographed by John Lloyd.

Chapter 8: Our wedding photograph was taken by our wedding photographer, whose name I, unfortunately, don't remember. It was taken in Oak Park, IL in 1988. The close-up of Hosain and me was taken by Tim Kellman.

Chapter 9: All four photographs in this chapter were taken by John Lloyd.

Chapter 10: The view camera was taken by John Lloyd. Hosain Mosavat took the four photographs of Fayette and the one of Spirit Island. Judy Mosavat took the photograph of Hosain Mosavat.

Chapter 11: John Lloyd took the photograph of Hosain and Judy.

Chapter 14: Judy Mosavat took the photograph of Hosain's Gravestone.

Don't just go by
Say 'Good Morning'
The word 'Good' is good
    and 'Morning' is the signature of a new dawn
Say that to friends
        flowers
        frogs
        and alligators
          if you're lucky to come across one

So, say 'Good Morning' as often as you can
    even in the middle of the night
That makes your night
    as shiny as the early morning sun

So
    'Good Morning'

Contents

How It All Began

Ginger Wiechers:

Have you ever seen someone's image (a photograph, a painting . . .) and felt that you must meet that person? You experience a compelling prompting to make the connection.

One afternoon, at a coffee house in Plymouth, Michigan, that I was privileged to be the steward of, I had this experience. Artist, Howard Weingarden, came into the 'Annex' and we began to share. I asked to see some of his pen and ink drawings, and among the art was the captivating face of Hosain Mosavat. I paused for a long time and knew that I must meet this man. It was a knock on the door of my destiny. I asked who this person was and I discovered it was a friend of his. There was no time wasted in making arrangements for Howard to invite Hosain and his extraordinary wife, Judy, to meet. Gratefully, they accepted, and that began all the love and the joy that ensued.

It was his face that drew me to him. My mother used to say, 'Dear, you're more than a pretty face.' To my dear friend, 'Hosain, you're more than a pretty face.' How could I have known he was a teacher, Sufi, poet, photographer and all around loving and creative genius–that he would add so much kindness and love to me and my life, that he would honor and bless the non-profit that I founded, that's so near and dear to my heart. Hosain and Judy are presents that keep warming my heart and SOUL with each new encounter, shared moments and treasured memories.

I will tell you, it felt like a reunion when the day came–not a first meeting. For those of you who hold a similar belief, it was a SOUL connection, kindred spirits so dearly and deeply familiar. In that moment, friendship began to blossom and love began to grow.

It has been my experience that few relationships in life are pure love, joy, happiness, sharing and caring. Few relationships celebrate each other and their work with unconditional support and love. Yet I count Hosain and Judy among those sacred few who have and are the blessing to me that I described. I sincerely hope that I have been for them, all they are to me.

Together we have brought more love to the world through poetry, photography, dinners, events and S.O.U.L. When I mentioned we have SOUL connection, I meant it literally and figuratively. I have the privilege to be the executive director of a non-profit organization, S.O.U.L., Source Of Universal Love (www.SourceOfUniversalLove.com). Through Hosain and Judy's graciousness, kindness, generosity and giving natures, they have supported and uplifted this organization with great love. They have been the perfect wind in my sails. For this and so much more, I am humbly and eternally grateful.

You can imagine that when the opportunity came to be part of sharing Hosain's story, so the world would have the opportunity to more fully know this remarkable, accomplished poet, author, photographer, chef, inventor, I recognized it is a once-in-a-lifetime experience. In putting together this love project, we included our dear friend, Babak, and we decided to bring in friends and family by asking for questions they might have of Hosain. So, this became a collection of the stories and memories of Hosain's life as told by him. Enjoy the journey and be prepared to be deeply touched and fall more in love.

Hosain:

I received a call from a person, who said, 'I am Ginger.' I said, 'I'm glad to meet you.' She said, 'I have just talked to a friend of yours who has asked me to get in touch with you, and I want to do that.' I asked, 'Why?' She said, 'I met Howard Weingarden and I saw your image, and also he told me that you were a poet.' She invited me to her coffee house to meet me. She asked me about my photography, which I asked about putting in her coffee shop. She immediately agreed to do that. When we hung the prints, I was supposed to go there and meet some people. So I did. And then she asked me to read some poetry, which I was glad to do. I said, 'You don't know what kind of poetry I write. My poetry may not be very good.' She said, 'It doesn't matter.' That's how it began—complete trust.

The Early Years

At the very beginning of the 1900s, my grandfather was a revolutionary in reaction to an earlier Shah called Reza Shah. He started an underground newspaper against that Shah and named it 'Mosavat,' which means 'equality.' At that time, he also changed the family name to 'Mosavat.' They hid him in the Shah's kitchen. The Shah wanted to drink his blood. He wanted to be in Tehran, but friends helped him escape to Germany in order not to be executed.

I was born with the name Sayyed Mohammad Hosain Mosavat. 'Hosain' means 'inner beauty.' 'Sayyed' means a descendant of the Prophet Mohammad. 'Tabataba'i' means both father and mother are descendants. That is true of me. My mother and father were cousins.

I was born in 1934 in Shiraz, Iran–the land of roses, poets and Shiraz wine. It is where Hafez and Saadi grew up to be giants of Persian poetry. So, I was sentenced to be a poet for the rest of my life. I was raised in Tehran. As I grew up, I realized my first and true teacher was my mother. I was the only and lonely child. I needed attention. In order to get that, I was able to learn Persian music with the aid of my mother. She was gentle, precious with everyone. All my family called her 'Mother.' I started writing poetry by taking a famous song and putting in my own words to make it sound funny. She sang poetry to put me to sleep, especially Rumi's, and later on taught me to create poetry, music, calligraphy and painting. When I was 15, she would read and interpret Hafez. From then on, I wanted to be a poet, a musician, a calligrapher, a painter and everything else I could put my heart into. She taught me that I could do anything, if I wanted it badly enough. When I was old enough to hold a Persian instrument called 'tar,' she taught me how to play it. I later became an accomplished tar player. The tar is the precursor to the guitar and sitar. And when I got older yet, she taught me painting. When I came to America, I lost my mother's enthusiasm and her teaching me painting. Going to school did not give me a chance to paint. Not knowing English, I took classes in mathematics and science. I knew the formulas from my high school years in Iran. Once I graduated and got a teaching job, I had no time for painting. I became a photographer as a result. And when the digital world came into the picture, I started painting digitally from my photographs. I woke up at almost 30 years of age to realize the seed of poetry she had planted in me, and writing heartfelt poetry became a part of my everyday existence.

It is my mother's love and love of poetry and music that have brought me here, together with her essence. She will never be apart from me, even though she departed over forty years ago. Those who know mothers will understand what my mother has meant to me. Seek your mother; appreciate the life she has given you. And never forget your father, who provided the space for your growth and endearment, for we're all what they made us.

With your own hands
    you carried me to where I am

With your lips
    you whispered me to sleep
You helped me to my first walk
My first laughter
    was at your face
My first word was 'Mother'

I am so sorry
    I was not with you to hear your last word
But that is OK now
I am playing the music you taught me years ago

My dear Mother
With your hands
    you are still carrying me today

My mother was the first person I ever loved. My father was my protector and a doctor. He built hospitals in Iran.

I went to school in Tehran and graduated from High School there. High School in Iran is six years. In 1953, two years before my graduation, the first Revolution in Iran against the Shah began. The violence was great. Within three days, a coup d'état happened, financed by the CIA, which I didn't survive because of losing fifteen friends. I also lost faith in my country. I felt unwelcome in my own country without freedom. I insisted on going to France. At that time, French was Iran's second language and everyone learned it in school. Now, English is the second language. My father thought I'd become a playboy if I went to France. So, he decided to send me to America; I had no choice. This was 1955. I was accepted at the University in Cookeville, TN and got a grant to go there. But there were only two places that had the English Language Institute for people who didn't know English, like me. They were in Washington, D.C. and Ann Arbor, Michigan. I picked Ann Arbor because of the University of Michigan. And because of immediately being in the University, I learned English in three months. In America, I finished my schooling. I got a B.S. in Mathematics & Physics, an M.S. in Mathematics & Physics and a Ph.D. in Physics (except for the dissertation). And I taught Physics and Mathematics at the high school level for 30 years.

Every death that I experienced in the Revolution made me appreciate the ones who were left. So, I began to love more the ones who I already loved; I began to love people I didn't know. And I began to share my life with them in an open way and that relieved me of a lot of the pain because I didn't keep it in there. It changed it. I knew, because of my first experiences in Iran, it was hard to do that. I could not bear it, so I had to leave the country. When I came to a new country, I needed to make friends. I remember I made friends with a Russian spy. He was learning English language. He was a general in the Russian army, defected to America and there were all kinds of FBIs around him to protect him. He was my classmate. We went to restaurants and we talked with our hands and the little English we knew. That was my first friend, even though we didn't understand each other. When you open your mouth, it calms you down.

During this time, I began to write poetry. I played music and I photographed extensively, traveling wherever it was possible and photographing as many places as I could physically go to. It is in

America where I have lived, worked and served to bring peace and harmony, trying to heal the pain and losses of my friends and my country.

I married 3 times, one son, David, from the first wife, no fruits from the second wife and, finally, my third wife, Judy, became the love of my life—the friend I had been looking for.

My hobbies have been photography, computers, traveling, poetry, music, woodturning, welding, cooking, friendship and laughing. I try to be funny when I'm not. I try to bring laughter to any tears. And I don't really care how crazy I am, as long as I bring laughter every chance I get.

I retired from teaching in 1993 and have been living in Whitmore Lake, Michigan.

When I was young, I not only was introduced to the creative side of life, I was a rebel rouser, which I guess is creative, too. I enjoyed playing tricks and doing things others didn't do. There was a gardener in Iran who grew hot peppers. He'd give you $5 if you ate one, so you knew they were hot. As a kid, I went to high school with a hot pepper in my hands. I'd shake everyone's hand and then watch when they touched their faces or eyes. I couldn't stop laughing. Everyone knew it was me, since I was the only one laughing.

I brought a bee to school. I tied a long thread around it. Then it would fly all around with me holding the other end. The kids would be screaming. It was funny—something to do.

In grade school I had a nail. One end was dull, with paper at the other end to look like an arrow. I shot it with the two tips of my forefingers. It went behind a guy's ear. He pushed it away like it was a mosquito.

I had a goat who I trained to go after people who bent over.

I'd be with friends in the balcony of a movie theater with a peppershaker and shake it over the people in the seats below.

I raised silkworms in Iran. I watched the little insects grow. It's fun to see them and play with them. I watched them build a cocoon, fed them leaves and I saw the life from the beginning to the end. They would eat only one kind of leaf. They would use the cocoon to continue their life.

I had a cat and a small brass bed that had very low current. I would 'electrocute' the cat, but it always came back for more.

My best friend, Mansur, was afraid of his hair falling out. I told him if you cut it, it'd grow more. So, we went to a barber. He went first. When he was done, I looked at him. He looked so ugly, I told him I'm not going to do that.

I had a Geometry teacher in high school who made jokes. When I answered questions, I was always making jokes and taking angles on what he said. The teacher was mad at me because I was funnier than him. So, the teacher would ask me the harder questions. I knew he would do that, so I was always ready.

In Iran, I had a friend who was a painter, who was wearing shoes without soles. I supported him, bought him some shoes, and he gave me some paintings. I met him through a friend of mine who was making signs–big signs. His name was Khosh Navis, which means 'beautiful writer.' At noon, we'd all get together and eat Dizi, which is a famous Persian stew. People put meat and vegetables in a clay pot in the early morning. They take it to the baker and the baker puts it in a Persian tanoor oven. Then at noon they go get it for lunch. It's a great get-together for people who work together. Khosh was also the neighbor to an acrobat, who would play at different clubs at night. The acrobat also made atr, Persian for perfume. His name was Attar or the 'perfume-maker.' He also performed at weddings, where he invited me to play my tar. He had a friend named Tutuni, which means 'a person who makes cigarettes.' Attar sometimes would take us to a brothel, where he would perform his acrobatics. We got caught in the brothel, which was illegal, punished by a fine. They asked him, 'Why are you here?' He said he was there to interview the prostitutes, although that wasn't true. But after that, he wrote a book called 'Come with Me to the House of Prostitution.' It was about the lives of the prostitutes from childhood to selling themselves for money. He was a famous man. He did not want to be caught in that position, and writing the book was his way out of the embarrassment. He was rich, he liked entertainment and he paid for everything–food, drink and all the rest.

Moslems do not keep dogs unless they are guard dogs or seeing-eye dogs. It's not illegal; they consider them unclean and untouchables. I picked up a friendship to an orphaned dog in the neighborhood that I liked very much. My father immediately forbid it and asked me to let it go. I asked my father, 'Why can't I keep it?' He said, 'The only dogs we keep are guard dogs.' My attachment to this friend was so deep, I couldn't bear to get away from it. I asked my friends at grade school about guard dogs. I understood that guard dogs must have good hearing and dogs with floppy ears cannot hear, therefore their guarding is limited. His ears flopped. So, I got a scissors, sat in front of the dog and proceeded to cut one of his ears. Good intentions, horrible experience. I was very young and ignorant. The dog started bleeding, bearing the hurt, yet standing, would not resist. I realized my ignorance and I stopped immediately. The lesson I learned from that dog is with me every day, which is a loving heart that we shared. I love the dog, who taught me forgiveness, and above all, who loved me. I see that dog every time I am near one. I was hurting the dog, yet he stood face-to-face with me and accepted me. It brought tears to my eyes and made me understand my ignorance. If I can be as loving as that dog, I will be a good person. My first lesson of love.

Sharon, my second wife, loved cats. I had bought her a cat from the Humane Society. She was so surprised when she walked in the house. She talked to the cat and called him Jamshid, who was one of the emperors in Persia. One of the things that first attracted me to Sharon was that she spoke Farsi! We never let him out; he was a house cat. During the divorce, she demanded that she wanted the cat. I said, 'OK.' After a few years, I asked her about Jamshid. When he went to Denver with my ex-wife, he fathered many, many cats–enough to kill him.

This was the cat that taught me love. He used to run so hard that his hind end got in front of him and he'd roll over. He loved to play with me. I grabbed his head with my hand, and he would put his paws around my hand while I was holding his head. And he would keep scratching me with his back paws. It got to a point that every time I reached for his head, he grabbed my wrist, which was on his face, with his front paws and his back paws scratching my arm–like fighting. But it was a peaceful fight–a game. Biting me without hurting me was his usual game. After a few months, I noticed some days he wasn't doing that. Then he couldn't walk and balance himself. I knew I had to take him to a doctor. The vet said he wouldn't live that long. He gave him a shot. He gave me pills to push down his throat. He told me to force feed him. Gradually, he found strength. He began to purr. I used to put him around my neck on the back of the couch. Then one day, he bit my ear. I knew he was alive and back. There was so much joy between me and the cat. And after he got well, he communicated with me by biting my face, which was telling me, 'I'm coming back. Thank you.' It was the most pleasure that I have got. It was a communication of care and love that was coming back from him. That's a feeling I will never forget.

I so much enjoyed him, loved him, that, at the time of the divorce, because I loved my wife, she had the right to keep Jamshid. It was a sacrifice. So, this was my first lesson of love from a cat.

I received a plant that bore jasmine flowers, with a story. When I was young and in Iran, my aunt used to put jasmine (yas) flowers on the table and sometimes string them around my neck. Since I was the oldest, I was the only recipient of such treatment. Then my aunt passed away and my cousin went to Iran for her funeral. He cut a few branches, put them in a plastic bag with some water and brought them back to America in Houston. I went to visit him in the 90s. I saw them and told him they were just like my aunt's flowers. He said they were, in fact, hers and told me how he brought them home. He gave me a few branches and told me how to take care of them. I kept cutting branches and growing new jasmines. I got so many of them. And during their flowering, people were impressed with how beautiful they smelled. So, I decided to share my aunt's flowers with friends. I told them how to take care of them and at the same time, I told them they must name them 'Muness.' That was my aunt's name. Unfortunately, I no longer have any of them because of my summer trips for photographing. I could not take care of them for extended periods of time, so I gave them away. I miss them very much. But I can visit a few of them across the street at our lucky neighbor's house.

I was not a good son. I did not like my father. He had many wives: 4 permanent ones, which was the legal limit, and over 103 temporary ones. [If you wanted to have sex in Iran, you had to get married, even for a night. A temporary marriage happened so that if the woman conceived, the man would also be responsible.] I have five brothers and four sisters, plus one sister who died as a baby. My youngest brother is 49 years younger than me. In Iran, we don't recognize half brothers and sisters; they're all brothers and sisters to us. Since I was the first and only child of my mother and father, my mother suffered a lot. Since my mother's feelings were hurt, naturally I didn't like my father. But while these feelings were going on, I also respected my father. He was a good physician; he was known almost everywhere and he built many hospitals. He was the only one the Shah trusted with money. So, he would go around, especially in southern Iran, and build hospitals, staff them, keep them running for a while, and then move on to another city to build another one. At one time, Ayatollah Khomeini asked him to be his Secretary of Health. My father refused. He said that where he worked, there were many sick and poor people; they needed him more than the Ayatollah did. At the same time, my father would invite a lot of religious people, so I wanted to be an old man, so he would respect me. I did get old, but he wasn't around then. Many of my father's visitors were darvishes, Sufis—people who were intelligent. I wanted to have a conversation with them and I wanted to be one, because he showed so much respect for them. But I wasn't behaving too well. To look at the older people, listen to them and never object to anything that comes to you. In other words, no rebellion—receive more, learn from them. And if you object, you actually stop any conversations that are beneficial. Then all you get is corrections. And when my father corrected me, that was pretty severe. He was also against me learning music and playing. I told him I no longer wanted to be in Iran after the Revolution of 1953. To my surprise, he agreed. That's when I came to America. One time, I was having an argument with my father. Afterwards, I heard him and my mother arguing about his treatment of me. He told my mother that I was his son; he needed to correct me because I was his son. He said he still loved me. That changed me instantly, and I closed the chapter on my father. I ran away to my grandmother's. She was the one I always went to.

When my father came to the U.S. to visit me, I was living with a young lady I wasn't married to. He asked me to marry her, because he was not allowed to look at her face without our being married. So, we had a little marriage ceremony and she gave me a dowry of $1. This is legal, according to my father's tradition. I photographed a nude friend. Her face was covered and I gave that to him. He was very upset. I told him he couldn't look at her face, so what's wrong? But he never returned that photograph.

In 1953 in Iran, I was invited to play music for a wedding, which was on a hilltop, out of town. My best friend, Mansur, who was a musician, and I played together many times. We were playing for this wedding. As we were playing, suddenly a group of plain-clothes police got all around us and took us all to prison. Mansur and I went to prison together. They left the women behind. They explained that we did not have the license to gather. Since the Revolution that year, there was a law that you could not have more than three people gather anywhere without permission. We were sent to a large detention room with many people sitting on the floor. I had a mustache. People who had mustaches were considered communist. When I entered the detention room, I was told to get rid of my mustache. All I had was a little clipper, and did what I could to cut it off. Some people were lying on their stomachs with others rubbing them with raw eggs to stop the bleeding. Apparently, they had been tortured. They would do this in batches and then send them back to the room we were in. And the effect was quite immense. No one knew when they would be called or how much whipping would be done. Anyone who wanted to use the bathroom had to go with a guard. Not knowing, I was walking faster than I should have and one of the guards with a bayonet hit me in the leg. I have a scar to this day. On the way to the police station, my cousin had seen me. He went to my father and told the story. My father immediately started searching for his people who could help me. I was let out after less than 24 hours. Mansur was let go the next day. I was released, but I had to sign a statement made by the police that I was a member of a forbidden group–that I had resigned and regretted being a part of it. Then they released me, and my statement was published in the newspaper. This was a CIA-run operation that brought the Shah back after the Revolution. From that day on, I no longer wanted to stay in that country. I firmly believed that I would not be safe to stay there. I did not go out and did not associate with anyone. Mansur came to America first; I came then after that. He went to Utah and graduated and went back to Iran and married my cousin; he passed away a few years ago. And I still see his son and his son's wife and daughter, who are very dear to me.

In my spare time in Iran, I was an unpaid fortune-teller. Someone came to our house as a guest. He was a magician. He put a nail through his tongue and many different things. And he used to read the palms of people. I thought: why couldn't I do that? So, I did. I asked people if anyone wanted me to tell their fortune. Fortunately, many people wanted to hear that. I looked at their hands, made up stories about the lines in their hands: their life line, their love line, how many kids they would have. You name it, I could read it. I had more fun than they did because they believed me. So, while I am writing this book, the person with me, Ginger, has asked me to read her palm. You're going to live a long life. You have a lot of sexability. And this line shows you had a broken heart and this is your heart line; you have a very good heart. (I'm just going with what I know about her.) And these three creases on the side of your hand represent your three children. You also have a line that says you have a lover. (She asked: What's his name? Answer: That's above my pay grade.) A free hand massage came with a small charge.

I also did hypnosis. Back in Iran, somebody came to our house. He was a hypnotist. I learned some from him. Back in America when I was a student, I learned some from others. I became good at it. Two weeks before the final exams, I would go to the Fraternity houses, hypnotize them to do nothing else but to study for their finals. I learned the power of suggestion and how strong it is. In one of my classes in graduate school, I wanted to give a lecture about the power of suggestion. It was a speech class. I asked the instructor if I could hypnotize the whole class. He said he needed to talk to the Dean of the school for permission. I wasn't given it. I asked the professor if I could bring my own person to hypnotize. He said that's okay. I proceeded to hypnotize him, took all of his feelings out of his hand and hit his hand as hard as I could. He didn't feel it and couldn't remember it when I woke him up. I got an A out of it. In that class, people gave speeches and everyone wanted to volunteer me to speak. My stories were so long, it didn't allow others time to give their speeches. Therefore, they got As because there was no time for them. On another occasion, I took a bunch of students to tutor for the final exam. I hardly slept that night. When we were taking the final exam, everybody aced it, except me. I fell asleep during the exam. I hadn't had any sleep. So, I got an E and everyone else got an A.

In college, I became sick. They put me in the student hospital. I had a final exam. They did not release me from the hospital, so I escaped, went to the class, got an E. Then I came back to the hospital.

In 1956, I was invited to Washington, D. C. by the Shah's daughter and her husband to be Master of Ceremony of a gathering of Iranian students in the U.S. As Master of Ceremony, I played tar and made jokes. I was always good at talking in front of big groups. I always made it feel intimate. But then mugs of coffee were thrown at the stage. I took my tar and ran behind the curtain. It was the beginning of the Revolution against the Shah, and students were showing their anger against the Shah's daughter and son-in-law. After that incident, I wanted to go to Iran to visit my family. My family advised me not to come. I asked them 'why not?' They had heard about what happened in Washington with the students, and they advised me not to come—that I would be arrested. I did go. No one was after me. I was free to go anywhere. No problems.

Since moving to America in 1955, I have gone back to Iran five times. I took my wife, Judy, with me in 2002 and 2005 to introduce my country to her. The last time I went was in 2005; most of my friends were gone. Some were so old I couldn't even recognize them. It was a good visit, but it did not feel like it was my home. It was a relief when I came back to America. I only got to visit the graves of my father and my mother and some friends. This finished the chapter of me being Iranian. My mother, my father, my friends and their influences still stay with me, and I'm grateful for what I have become with their teaching and sacrifice. Sometimes reality is unreal. I did not lose a single step by becoming a U.S. citizen. I have more friends; I've learned an immense amount through life experiences of people and places, from beautiful to ugly. You should have been with me at my 80th birthday party to see how many friends I have who have well respected me, loved me and shared my heart in return with their hearts. Some friends around the fire stayed until morning. I was too tired to stay up. I could honestly say I have become far more compassionate and loving to everyone because of Iran. The freedom, the relationships, the honesty, the care have been unbelievable. Although we march, we burn, we demonstrate, we slaughter people here, still it's far better than where I have been. No matter how bad it is, I still believe this country is better than anywhere else.

Father

My first marriage, to Betty, was very short, very unhappy. In the second week of my marriage, I was going to school. Didn't have any time or money. She was on the phone calling a friend in Chicago. I asked her, since we didn't have much money, she shouldn't talk too much. She kept talking, so I went and hung up the phone. She got the phone away from me and slammed the phone so hard, it fell off the wall. That was the second week of our marriage. That marriage ended right there. We went to a marriage counselor; didn't work. But I was determined to stay married.

Later on, I found out she was pregnant. On the day of my son's birth, I had a final exam. I did not go to the exam. The professor asked me why I didn't show up. I said I was witnessing my son's birth. He didn't believe me and gave me an E. I felt very happy at his birth. I couldn't wait to come home and hold him. I was living in Dexter, going to school in Ann Arbor. When I held him, I felt like I was holding my whole future. I got a cat for him. It was his companion. They played a lot. I couldn't afford the apartment in Dexter, so I moved. I had to quit school, save my tuition money so we could pay the rent. She realized that we could not continue, so she got a job at University of Michigan Hospital. This allowed me to go back to school the next semester. I wanted to stay with her because of my son, David. The marriage counselor we were seeing said we should spend more time together. I wrote a letter to my mother asking her to come from Iran, so she could sit with David, so Betty and I would have more time together. That did not work. So, I sent my mother back.

Then I decided I needed to end the marriage. I moved out. Every time I went to see David, once a week, when I left him, he was screaming so hard because he did not want to stay there and didn't want me to leave. I hated to go see him and hear him scream. To this day, I hate screaming.

So, I did not go see him in order not to see him suffer like that. His mother and I divorced after three years of marriage.

I think I've never felt as bad as when I couldn't make the marriage work. It's not that I was no longer married; it was that I was no longer with David. It was a pretty bad time for me. In college, in order to pay my bills and child support, I went to school during the day and had two jobs. I took the afternoon shift at St. Joseph Hospital's Sanitarium. During the midnight shift I was an ambulance driver for University of Michigan Hospital staff, plus going to school. So, I had no time to sleep. When a member of the university needed an ambulance, I'd drive the ambulance with medical assistants to get them. The ambulance driver is also in charge of the morgue. My job was to sit in a booth and wait for someone to come to claim a body. I had to find the body in a drawer of the cooler, check the number and get a receipt from them, and then they'd take the body. There was maybe one ambulance call. There were more calls for the morgue than for an ambulance. Not a lot of work, so I slept in the morgue.

When David was young, maybe 9 or 10 years old, his mother threw a birthday party for him. She had some balloons to tack to the wall. He pulled a balloon off the wall and the tack went into his eye. In about two years, he was completely blind in that eye.

I went to his grade school when he was playing baseball, so I'd see him from a distance. One time he called me and told me that he wanted to come and see me. I said okay, I'd come to get him. When I drove to Saline to get him, he had a bag and was walking almost to Ann Arbor, about 10 miles away. I took him to the police station and told them that where he lives, he doesn't want to be. They didn't do anything. They said since his mother had custody, which is how it was done back then, there was nothing they could do. Not seeing me a lot hurt David. And she would not talk about me to David without anger. After a while, David began having some really harsh feelings for me, and I just accepted it and went to see him as often as I could.

His anger was so much, it took years before I could make him understand that I could not live with his mother. He was completely on his own. He got into drugs. His stepfather kept helping him, and still helps him to this day. There was a man in his life that cared for him. He kept him alive. And he got him off the drugs and he's clean. He didn't get over the anger for a lot of years. I felt helpless because he wasn't near. His mother passed away in 2005.

He got jobs cooking at restaurants, painting houses and remodeling houses. He got married for a couple of years, living in Dearborn, Michigan. That marriage did not last long and he moved to St. Petersburg, Florida, where he remodels houses. I went to see him a couple of times. He has one dress code: painter overalls that he never gets out of. I think I bought him ten painter overalls. I offered to buy him a house, which I did. I gave him the ownership of the house free and clear. I bought him a commercial smoker and gave him our four-wheel-drive truck. The smoker and truck are for when David can no longer remodel houses. He loves to cook and to grill, like me. He can use it as a type of food truck down in Florida. His mother was also a cook and opened up a restaurant in Ann Arbor called 'Granny B's,' so he got it from both sides. On weekends, he BBQs for almost the whole neighborhood. Everyone loves him and gets around him. I also bought him a large TV, so when his friends got around, they could look at the games and whatever they wanted to watch. Got him a satellite dish. I shall continue to get him things he enjoys, and my enjoyment is to see him happy. He trusts me, and when he promises me, he goes through with it. And he trusts me that if I say something, I will do it. And whenever he needed help, I was there. I miss him very much. I only have this one son. I found the value of my son in my life, and I felt his happiness, which made me happy. I knew what fatherhood was. I'll never be alone. I have a son and an angel as my wife.

David calls her 'Mom.' If I have anything negative to say about Judy, he jumps and calms me down and says, 'You don't do that.' That was early in our marriage. Now that we have shown David how much we love each other, he's secure. And if he wants to talk about his life and his problems, he talks to her. She loves him as her son.

Musician

My mother started me playing music. She had a tar (the precursor to the guitar and sitar) that she played and she taught me how to play. When I got interested, it was through a Sufi during the Iranian Revolution in 1953. We were fighting against the Shah and, for our own safety, every night, my friends and I gathered together to spend time as a group for safety. One of the masters of music was playing sitar. He was a Sufi. He was singing, and then breaking down and crying, and then singing the same song again. But he wasn't able to finish the song. We were all laughing at him because he was unable to finish the song. And then, after awhile, we were all crying. The song he sang went, 'The only thing shared between us is my broken heart and your broken promises.' Finally, we fell asleep. That's when I became really interested to become as expressive as he was. He was a master musician, who composed our revolutionary song. That's when I began to play as hard and as expressive as he was: Ostad Malek, sitar and santour.

Because I was funny in telling quick jokes, people invited me to mass gatherings as a Master of Ceremony. I would tell jokes, play music and entertain with other people who were musicians. A master tar player was playing in nightclubs. He asked me to accompany him and taught me many songs. Then he asked me to play on Iranian radio. He mentioned my name as one of the musicians. One of my aunts heard that and she called me and said I was forbidden to play music. She said if I do, don't mention my name. It becomes a family shame. Being a musician was a shameful thing at that time in Iran. A certain class of people were musicians–a lower class. Later on, it became important and a lot of people loved music. So, I was kind of depressed. I was very proud of myself, then this came to be. But I kept inviting musicians to my house. We played all night long. Many master musicians participated.

Interestingly, in Iran, I had the lucky occasions to play in houses of ill repute. I had a friend who was a master tar player. He had his own orchestra. We became friends and he would play on different occasions, like birthdays, weddings and whorehouses. We played dance music, in particular, belly dancing, where half-naked belly dancers danced around and offered their breasts to put money in their crevices.

I had some teachers who taught me how to play dombak, which is a Persian hand drum. I really liked playing drums, so when I came to America, I took a wood shop class, glued layers of mahogany together and turned my first drum. I still have it.

When I came to America in 1955, I only brought my tar. The frets were catgut and the strings were metal. And by playing a lot, the catgut broke. I made a plastic, fiberglass tar and a sitar with metal frets and kept playing them till my woodturning disabled my hands from too much vibration.

I made a santur, the real hammer dulcimer, which was tunable. I wanted to learn how to turn hand drums. I took some workshops with David Ellsworth, a master woodturner, who started the American Association of Woodturners, which became international. First, I turned the smallest goblet, which he thought was a winner, and then the longest goblet, which broke the record.

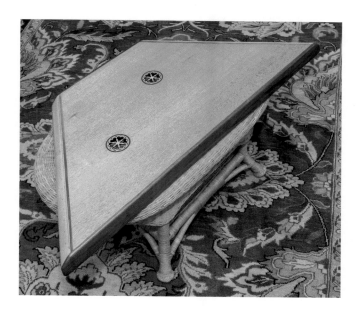

Because the hand drums I was turning were so big and no commercial lathe was able to do the job, I made my own lathes, one for inside the shop and one for the outside. Both were 5' in diameter. The outside one was used to take the bark off and clean it up. Then it was taken into the inside lathe to finish it. The one on the outside that took the bark off destroyed my knuckles with its vibration. I ended up stopping turning and stopping selling them. They were sold for $800 to $1000 apiece. This was in the 1990s.

Because I could no longer make them, I went to Washtenaw Community College to learn how to weld and began to build steel drums. I played and sold them. I used to have people around to play drums. I also went to drum circles. I seemed to attract a lot of musicians in Iran and throughout my life and to this day.

I had musicians who had difficulty playing from their hearts. They had to have sheet music to play from. I was not able to accompany them. I was playing free by feelings; they were playing by music sheet, so I could never accompany them. My musical friends insisted that I must learn how to read music, which meant my heart had to leave me to go on a piece of paper, which was foreign to me and unacceptable.

I have a friend, Michele, who's a master violinist. Musically, he grew up in a symphony in Sicily and was traditionally trained. After knowing him for a while, I told him to let go and play from his heart. It was like a bird set free from his cage. To hear him play now is like a journey to the heavens.

Athlete

In the late 50s, when I was in college, I had to take classes in Physical Education. Swimming was best for me. I took a Red Cross test to become a lifeguard. And I took another class about training lifeguards. In the summertime after college, I became a lifeguard at Groom's Beach, Whitmore Lake, MI. I saved some people from drowning. Once a week I used to cook for the lifeguards. I was a head lifeguard. It was okay in the beginning, but the more I sat in the sun, the darker I got, and some people complained. Mr. Groom asked them to leave. I did this for several summers.

In the early 70s, I ran on Whitmore Lake Rd., a road that connects Whitmore Lake and Ann Arbor. People would try to run me off the road, calling me "communist." Later on, they recognized me and saw I was a good guy.

I also enjoyed fishing down the river in my canoe. Luckily, no one objected to that.

I was a boxer in Iran. To train for that you need to run. I met another Iranian boxer in Ann Arbor Bank. He had boxed in the Olympics in Iran. He was a physician and wanted to associate with me. This was 1970; he was the first Iranian I had met in America. We started talking about exercise, training, and decided we would start running together. We joined the YMWCA (Young Men and Women's Christian Association) in Ann Arbor and did some boxing. Too much work. So, we decided to run together. He could only run with me on weekends. But I kept running after school in Edward Hines Park. I joined Vic Tanny. I would go every day after work, run in Hines Park, which was right behind Vic Tanny in Plymouth, MI. I got some of my co-workers to join me. We'd go to work, then go to run to get rid of the frustrations of the day. Then we'd go to Big Boy and eat most of the salad bar. Dr. Fazlollah Nickhah, the man I met in the bank, was president of the Midwest American Association of Sports Medicine. He told me he wanted to run the Boston Marathon, but he didn't think he could do it. I made him a promise, that if he would run, I would run with him. I was hoping he wouldn't run, but he did. And so did I. He was four years older than me; ran faster than me. My best time in Boston was 3 hours and 27 minutes. His was better, I think by a half hour. We ran our first time in 1976. We ran again in 1977.

There is a parallel story here. I met Tom Silvia on an indoor track in the Track and Tennis building of U of M in 1975, where I was running for running's sake. I saw this skinny, long-haired, good-looking young man, who kept running by me once too many times. I yelled at him, 'Have you no respect for your elders? Could you run with me for a while so I could feel better?' Of course, I was joking, but he slowed down, ran with me less than a mile, and we became friends for 32 years, until his physical heart gave out. His true heart never has. He ran with me almost every day from then on. He came to Whitmore Lake, where I lived, and ran with me. He actually trained with me to run a marathon. Then he invited me to the world's #1 race–the Boston Marathon. He said, 'My parents live in Hopkinton, Mass., where the race begins and my brother will pick us up where the race ends.' And I could stay at his parents for the duration. Beautiful parents, great host. We ran together twice at the Boston Marathon. He did not mind leaving me behind in his dust, and I did not mind keeping his friendship for revenge. I went to his brother's wedding. I went to his wedding. Then he was nowhere to be seen. I saw him twice more, fortunately, within a year before he died. It was so joyful to see him, for the best part of my life was spent chasing him on the tracks. I saw myself young again in his eyes with the stories he remembered about us with strong hearts, red faces and sweating profusely, sometimes for hours, on weekends. He made me believe I could do a marathon. That is not an everyday event. Since that day I finished my first Boston Marathon with him, I have been a different person with a touch of his heart carved in me. It says, 'You can do it.' Also, I read my poetry to him and he made music to my poems. He was a great musician.

Running is addictive. It's called 'euphoria' when you run a long time. I kept running about 10 miles a day for years. I had no time to date anyone or associate with anyone. I became vegetarian and stopped dating. No one would come to Vic Tanny and wait for me to finish. That's when I became celibate—until I met Judy in a poetry reading of local Ann Arbor poets. In a few months, she took all my pride, and my virginity went right out of the window. Best thing that ever happened to me. That was over 30 years ago. She is still beside me, and she has kept me alive many times. I wish there were more Judys around. I could use another five. After 30 years, I still hold her hand on my chest when I go to sleep. And Fazi, as I called my dear friend, lived to be 84 years old.

Chef

My early collegehood was faced with lack of money. Every time I walked from my classroom to the dormitory, I smelled food at the dormitory. We were served peanut butter and jelly in the cafeteria–mostly at lunch. I wanted to change this situation. I had an Iranian friend, who was working at Tappan International House, a sorority at the U of M, in which only girls would live there and Fred, who worked in the kitchen for his meals. I was able to work for my meals, too, by being the sous chef for the cook in the sorority. For me to go to school and pay child support for the son I had from my first wife, having free lunch and dinner was a great source of income.

Another source of income was owning the Fleetwood Diner in Ann Arbor for 10 years in the 60s. It's been a 24-hour-a-day institution and is still open today.

During my first marriage, my mother came to visit and taught me how to cook Persian food. My mother loved to cook. We had a cook, but she was not allowed to cook. My father sometimes had a lot of guests. Then the cook would prepare the meals. So, when my mother came to America, I took advantage of her. The housemother of the sorority was called Mrs. Griffey–a black beautiful lady, who took me in as her son. In order to repay her, I suggested, 'Why don't I cook some Persian food on weekends at Tappan International House?' So, then I was making Persian food. Volunteered to cook on the weekends. And she taught me how to cook in volume. The girls who were living there would invite boyfriends and other friends, and I would cook Persian food for them. Somewhere between 30 to 50 people would show up, eat Persian food and be grateful.

One of the guests was Sharon, who became my second wife. She sat at my table and talked Farsi to me! That impressed me that she knew so much about Iranians and was able to talk to me in Farsi. Being without money, I wasn't too social and couldn't go out. So, we met at the

Michigan Union a few times, and things began to start on the road to marriage. She was granted a Fulbright Scholarship from a famous senator. She got a job as a teacher and I got a job as a teacher. And when I started teaching, once a year I would have a Persian night and cook for all the teachers and their friends. I also entertained them playing tar and bringing carpets and jewelry and things that were Iranian, to show the culture. I also played drums and told jokes. I also invited the superintendent of the school. Sharon got fired 3 times. I told her, in that case, I would send her to school to get her Ph.D. After one semester, I realized she spent more time at school and almost zero time at home. I sat her at a table facing her. I said, 'Either go to school and we separate or if you want me, you have to quit school.' She said, 'I need some time to think about it.' I gave her 30 days. At the 30th day, I asked for an answer. She said, 'I will not quit school.' I said, 'Well, you are going out of this house right now.' She went to a friend of mine's house and lived there. Her father and mother came to Ann Arbor and took her back to Colorado. I divorced her and gave her everything she wanted and thanked her for clarifying my future. I still see her whenever I go to Colorado. She sends me birthday cards and we respond in kind. I consider her a friend of mine.

I was running, wanted to improve my time for the Boston Marathon. I had to be able to run 26.2 miles in under 3½ hours to qualify. A friend suggested if I turned vegetarian, I would lose some weight and gain speed. So, I went to a class at the YMWCA (Young Men and Women's Christian Assn.) and learned how to cook vegetarian food. The teacher was from India. I learned to love hot food. We students, once a month, got together to cook Indian food. It went on for a few months, then it slowed down and hardly anybody came. But I kept on doing it on my own and invited other people. For that and many other reasons I had acquired many friends. Then I invited Ann Arbor Camera Club members for a picnic at my home once a year in June. Then later the Woodturners Club and welders at Washtenaw Community College, where I took welding classes, to come for a 230 lb. pig roast in a roaster, which I made at WCC.

I was a vegetarian for 21 years. But I wasn't a strict vegetarian. To me, friends came before diet. If someone invited me to their home, I'd eat whatever they served me. I honor my friends and family and would never tell them 'no.' So, I was a vegetarian on my own time.

In Iran as a child, my mother and I travelled to get some vegetables. I still remember how gentle and proud the gardener was to offer the best of his garden. With a knife, cutting very gently, he made room for new vegetables to grow, flowers to offer and joy of life to share. In making room for new growth, he showed his love for the vegetables and flowers. And he spoke about the vegetables–the benefits, the remedies for different illnesses or different tastes, and the meaning of his flowers. Over 70 years ago, I still remember. A half hour of visiting the gardener and his garden has been my companion ever since–working with nature, nurturing it and offering it. That's the kind of love I have learned from.

I've since grown my own gardens–vegetables, herbs, roses. I had 80 tomato plants, watermelon, cucumbers, green onions, sweet green peppers and many other vegetables. Once I planted them, I'd go on a trip and the neighbors would pick whatever was ready. I always wanted to grow things, but then I found out it took a lot of time and work to kill the worms and get up early in the morning, and yet I wasn't there to enjoy the fruits of my labor. So, after a year or two, I gave it up. Then after a 40-year rest, I decided to grow hot peppers–and I mean hot! I grew Ghost peppers, Devil's Tongue peppers and Trinidad Moruga Scorpion peppers, which are the hottest peppers in the world. I pickled them in my homemade red wine vinegar and set them on a table and only looked at them.

This brings me to my homemade red wine vinegar. A dear friend of ours, Sarah, gave us a vessel with a vinegar mother in it, which is from a long line that has been around for over 150 years old. You put red wine in it. After 6 weeks, the wine becomes vinegar. An unfortunate accident happened. I fell on my back. The vessel fell and broke. But I had a bottle of the vinegar reserved, which I was using for cooking. That's all I had. After awhile I saw some things happening in the red wine vinegar. I thought it was a baby of the mother. I put that in another vessel with a bottle of wine. I developed another mother. Every 6 weeks, I kept putting another bottle of wine in to replace the original one, leaving some wine in it. Now I have lots of red wine vinegar made out of a 150-year-old line of mothers.

I also canned many boxes of garlic vinegar. It's a Persian treat, called Sir Torshi, which you wait at least two years for it to age and be ready to eat, but the longer, the better. You fill a canning jar with garlic cloves with the skin on or off. Then cover it with vinegar. We made so much with friends, that we still have boxes of cans from 1997! That garlic is just like soft butter, and we use the vinegar with oil for salad dressing.

I also concocted a delicious dessert–very simple. You cut a sweet, cold, seedless watermelon into bite-sized pieces. Sprinkle rose water on it evenly and gently stir. Refrigerate for at least a few hours in a baggie so you can mix it easily from time to time. I call it Rose Water Melon. Judy thought it was a Persian treat, so when we went to Iran, she looked for it and asked about it. No one had heard of it. She discovered that it was my invention. She said, 'If it's not Iranian, it's Hosainian!'

[This is from Michael, a dear and longtime friend of Hosain's:

You know, Hosain was never one to avoid excess in anything about which he was passionate. I recall showing up for a small gathering at a mutual friend's house. Hosain said he would handle the main dish–something chicken, something Iranian. I looked at the big aluminum pot and asked how many chickens he was cooking. He directed his sparkling brown eyes straight at mine and said, '40.']

My relationship to food is gathering friends, making friends, since food has no religion or politics. Everyone enjoys food, especially tastes from other countries.

My favorite meal is rice and Ghormeh Sabzi, which is a Persian herb and beef or lamb shank stew. The rice is basmati and is made with a golden crust. Delicious!

My favorite dessert is fruits, specifically pomegranates, grapes, cherries and melons. Growing up, we didn't have desserts. We had appetizers, which were pita bread, Persian cheese (similar to feta), walnuts, sabzi, which is green herbs, onions and radishes. When people came to visit, we offered them Shirini, which are delicious pastries.

In preparing for this book, I was asked, 'What advice do you give a person who says, 'I can't even boil an egg'? I said, 'Lay down and die.'

Many times, we gathered friends and family for an event in our Kolbeh (Farsi for Spiritual Nest–a gathering place in our back yard with a roof and posts and no walls, centered around a fire pit I put together–like a gazebo). I made it with the help of Judy and David and many of my woodturning friends. And I thanked them with one of the most delicious meals I made on one of the grills in the Kolbeh.

For any event, I start by welcoming everyone with a hug. That opens up everyone. If there's anybody new, I make sure to get near them and talk with them, make them feel welcome and comfortable. I normally tell a joke, because I find laughing opens their heart and they're closer. This is an art that is built into me. I wouldn't know how to do it any other way. I used to prepare Persian food. But that was difficult when it got to be more than 10 or 20 people. When I cooked in the school kitchen or sorority house, they had big kitchens, so I could cook a lot more Persian food. At home with private guests and friends, I'd smoke ribs and brisket. At times I've made hamburgers on the grill, corn on the cob, soaked in salt water beforehand and then grilled. When there were more than too many people, then I would roast a pig. I made a pig roaster that held a whole 230 lb. pig. And the party would be open and people could come any time and eat any time. There was always more than enough food. Then they would have to take it home.

I also had a 6-gallon African Dutch Oven. I built a crane to hold the pot over the fire. And sometimes I cooked chilies and some kind of a stew—anything that could boil for a long time. We used to gather in an all-night-long party with community cooking. Everyone who came must bring food: vegetable, meat and any stewing elements. If anyone came without it, we'd send them to the grocery store or they'd have to go home. We put all their ingredients into the pot and I donated water and spices—the hotter, the better. I found that they'd complain of the heat, but kept on eating. We let it cook all night until breakfast. Everyone slept out in the Kolbeh. If it turned out bad, it was the poor guests' fault. But that never happened, because the enjoyment of making it and putting it together was so much fun. Musicians played music, singers sang, joke tellers had fun, poets shared.

I was told my rib rub is to live for and was asked to share my masterpiece recipe. Some brown sugar, salt, pepper, turmeric, coriander, sour salt—in other words, open your spice cabinet and put everything and anything in it. And then rub all of this on the ribs and brisket. I take a torch and go over it a few times to give it a little burn and it makes it go into the ribs to infuse the flavor.

Then on the back of the ribs, I crisscross them with my knife–I don't peel it off. I also have a sauce that is separate–a not-so-secret Hosain's BBQ sauce. Cut a lemon in half. Put it in a pan. Put enough apple cider vinegar in it to boil the cut lemon. You could put chopped onions and garlic into it after softening and boiling everything out of the lemon. When it gets soft, you add the spices to it. Again, of your own choice–the best spices you can put into it. Then I'll take the lemon out. I normally add my own spices, which include cumin, turmeric, fenugreek, hot pepper, salt, sugar; whatever I look at and feels right, I put in it. I add Stubb's BBQ sauce to make it a thicker consistency. And then I simmer it for a long time. Then I put some cornstarch in it to thicken it to a point where you slide your finger on the back of a spoon. When it stays in place, it's thick enough. It's personal–thick or thin.

I was also asked to share my recipe for the Best-Ever Pork Belly. My secret is to share it. You put any spices of your choice–salt, cayenne pepper and lots of sour salt are mine–on the fat side. Sour salt is a burning agent, so put it under the grill, fat side up. Broil it until it's hot. Then throw it away towards friends.

This book could never be complete without discussing potatoes. I start with cutting the potatoes and putting them in the microwave. And while the microwave is going, in a big caste iron skillet, I sauté onions and garlic with sour salt and jalapeno peppers in duck fat. I put turmeric in it and Creole seasoning. I lower the heat and add the potatoes, mix them up and let them brown on one side. When they're browned and crispy, I turn them over and brown the other side. At this time, I add some lime juice. And if it is too dry, I add a little chicken broth. Be prepared to enjoy this delicious recipe.

I learned how to cure salmon in a class I took. I add brown sugar and salt, equal amounts, and fresh herbs, which I put in the food processor. While it's going, I put some Bourbon in it. I lay out the salmon fillets, flesh side up. I put the concoction on the salmon with my hands and rub it on all sides of the fish. Then I cut lemon rings, put them on top of everything on the flesh side. Then I put the 2 flesh sides together and lay them on a tray. Then I put another tray on top of it with a weight on it. When the fish squeeze together, the juice with all the herbs and Bourbon and spices replaces the juice of the fish, and the curing process happens. Put it in the refrigerator for 2 or 3 days. After 3 days, you take them out and rinse everything off of it–both sides. Put them on paper towels, pat dry and then cut it into portioned pieces. I vacuum pack them and freeze whatever I won't be eating right away.

I took a class at Washtenaw Community College. I learned to boil the vegetables to get all the funny things out of them. Then I put them in the canning jars. I put only the top seal on the jars. On the stovetop, I placed a large pan with a rack on the bottom with water that goes about halfway up the jar. I put the jars on the rack in the water, covered the pot and boiled it about 10 minutes. Then I lifted off the cover. That's when you hear the clicking of the sealing on the jars. Sometimes if it doesn't click, you can tap it with the end of a spoon to nudge it closed. Carefully put each jar on the counter with the retaining ring loosely screwed on. It can be screwed a bit tighter later.

I want to tell you the story of my mother's Torshi. My mother was well known in the family for her Torshi. Every family had its own Torshi recipe, handed down through the generations. When she came to visit me, I learned from her how to do that. Torshi is a condiment, usually made of eggplant and herbs, garlic, hot pepper and apple cider vinegar. The only source of spicy heat in Iran was the Torshi. And the degree of heat was up to the maker. Normally, green or red whole peppers were used. Mostly it was eaten with stews or soup.

This book is a continuous offering of recipes to keep me alive. So, if you like my recipes, please share them.

Your beloved chef,
Hosain

Teacher

I wanted to be a Nuclear Physicist. At the time that I graduated from the University of Michigan with a Bachelor's Degree, searching for nuclear jobs, I found I was not qualified because I was not a citizen, I wasn't born in the U.S. and those jobs were so-called 'classified jobs.' So with all the physics and mathematics classes I took, I thought I would go into teaching. But I had to have certain special classes to qualify to teach, like being a student teacher. That's when I went to Eastern Michigan University, because they trained people to teach. I was hired as a teacher at Garden City High School in Garden City, Michigan in 1963. I taught Mathematics and Physics for 30 years.

I was raised in a family of teachers. The only oddball was my father, who was a physician. When I was in high school, I used to teach music to my classmates. And whenever I had a chance to sit with a master, I became a good student. In college, I used to teach mathematics and physics to my classmates. I used to teach hypnosis and poetry, too. I also taught swimming. In my teaching classroom, I used to teach how to solve challenging puzzles, and I myself learned impossible puzzles to challenge my very best students so that they would become humble, and I invited them to bring puzzles to me that were most difficult.

When my mother wanted to come to visit me in the 1960s, she was told she could not go to America because she had insufficient ties to Iran, which means she might stay in America. I was very sad, almost in tears, when I went to the classroom the next day. The students asked me what was happening. I told them. They got angry, got together and made a petition to the State Senate. Three months later, my mother was granted permission to come visit me for the last time. Everyone in that school signed it. I will always be grateful to them.

I was put on three years' probation at Garden City High School. After two years of probation, they would give you tenure. They did not give me tenure. They tried to fire me many times. I fought the administration and went to the Garden City Teachers' Grievance Committee and got tenure. That didn't set well with the administration.

Eventually, I became head of the Office of Professional Responsibility. All grievances went through me. I was also president of the Garden City Federation of Teachers—the head of the Union in Garden City, Michigan.

I love to learn how to be pure. Little children bring that to me. I talk to them, ask them simple questions and make them see an image and ask them to write about it. They write something about it; I write an answer to them. Then I ask them to continue writing their own story. For example, how many flowers did you see on your way home? Did any friendly dog chase you home? Did you see a cat saying hello to you? Did you feel any friendship? Tell me how beautiful they were. Do you learn everything only in a classroom or observing nature on the way home? On one occasion, we went to see some relatives in Canada for the last time. Their young daughter, Anna, kept showing interest in me. Maybe it was the way I looked; I had a long beard. So, I took advantage of it. I asked her if she was able to write poetry. She said 'No.' Will you believe me if I say something? She said 'Yes.' So, I gave her a short poem. She said that's beautiful. I said to her she can do more beautifully than me. I said 'Try it.' She came up with some. In order for me to open her up, I said that was beautiful; I want more. She said 'But you're leaving.' I said 'No, I'm here. All you have to do is email me and I'll email you back.' We said that and said good-bye. It was a couple weeks later when I wrote her 'Where are you, Anna. Have you forgotten me?' She said 'No, I have not,' with a poem. I responded back. A few times after that, she was writing poetry, and her school published it with other students' work and her father sent the book to me. I said to her, 'I would like to have a picture of you. Please have your Dad send one to me.' It never developed and I was sorry that she was lost in her school activities.

Judy's niece's name is Julia Rose. I called her Rose. I started writing poetry with her when she was about 8. One time we went out to a park and sat on a bench. She would write poetry and

I would write a response. After about a half an hour, she stood up and said, 'Hosain, you have to learn something about children. They can't sit down too long.' So she ran around and came back for more.

[Hi, this is Judy, Hosain's wife. I want to share an experience Hosain and I had in a restaurant once. At the table next to us were two parents and their 9-year-old son, celebrating his birthday. Hosain leaned over towards the boy, beard and all, and said 'I was 9 once, and look what happened to me!' You should've seen the boy's eyes!]

While I was teaching high school, before every exam every Friday, I'd tell the students a funny story, like if they laughed, they would do better on the exam. The principal complained that I should teach mathematics and nothing else. I shared poetry in the classroom and the principal did not think that was proper either, so I changed it to camelosophy. So, before the tests started, I told camelosophy. Camelosophy was the philosophy of camels, which wasn't poetry or trying to change opinions or political. I made them laugh and then they took their exam. When they graduated from my class, they went to another class. On the days of the exams, they would not take their exam unless I came to their class and told them camelosophy.

I also taught the students how to say 'hi.' Normally, they would raise their hand in the air and say 'hi.' I'd put my hand down by my side and wave it, saying 'low.'

When I was teaching in the 1960s, a friend and fellow teacher grew a beard. I really liked it. I saw him one afternoon and it was gone. I asked him why. He said the administration told him he had to shave it off. From that day on, I didn't shave. Needless to say, the Administration didn't like me having a beard. I told them that if they had any problem, I'd see them in court. One day there was a fire alarm. The kids left and wouldn't come back. I brought them back in. After that, the teachers left me alone about my beard. The students, and even their parents, through the PTA, stood up for me in different ways. They loved me because I loved their kids. I can never forget their efforts and kindness.

Outside of school, I would bike with my students, riding from Garden City to Ann Arbor–a distance of 30 miles. We'd sit around and eat hot dogs with onions and hot mustard. I thought it'd slow their eating down, but it didn't. I also took them camping at Island Lake. The school didn't like it, but they didn't really have a say outside school. A couple of the students came with their parents. Sometimes my friends would come with guitars and drums and play for the students. We'd go around the campground to each campsite and those people would join us until 10:00.

My favorite part about being a teacher was to witness the growth of the young ones in the subject and in acceptance of who they are, what they like and always encourage communication exchange. Sometimes I share poetry. I ask their opinion all the time. And I find exchange and communication creates a special relationship, and some of them have become my lifetime friends.

I was a teacher for 30 years. I've been retired since 1993. I still remember the faces, expressions, disappointments and successes. I wish I could be there today and see if there was any footprint of my love in them.

I have seen some of them. They have changed. Their purity has been compromised. I want to be with them to guide them and grow with them. I could learn a lot from them. They have a lot of energy and the new look of this life. Today the problems they have are much more difficult than we had. They could teach me a lot and I would love that. I'm afraid those days are gone. And I'll be gone too. But that's the story of life.

I will always be a teacher by looking at my life and thanking the people who taught me.

Husband

I have someone to share with you—a soul mate, a friend, a lover, a wife—all wrapped in one, which I call my Mother. You see, motherhood is not just giving birth, giving milk and changing diapers. It is about creating and forming the future life of a person you care about. It's about holding hands, walking step by step to newer and higher places at every possible moment. Her name happens to be Judy, but that is an insult; it is a four-letter word. She is a collection of quadrillions of touching moments—from the moment I met her, to when I was on my back fighting to live, to my triumphs of publishing books and taking photographs. I am, at this moment, who she made me. Without her, I would probably have not survived. And I want you all to know where I come from. My natural Mother got me started, and my spiritual Mother will finish it. I'm grateful to Judy forever, and whatever comes after.

There is not a word that has been created to show our relationship. Let me put it in a very simple image: How would a ceiling survive without the walls? In other words, I exist because of her.

I am most proud of Judy. I never go anywhere without her. She's always with me—not only physically, but also emotionally. And I get up early in the morning, waiting to hug her and say 'Good Morning.' She shows her heart to me, her closeness and buries her face in my beard, even though it's difficult to breathe. The whole world belongs to me then.

Judy, my last and only wife, became the backbone of my creativity. This is where the first book of my poetry came from. She inspired it, typed it, chased publishers, begged friends and borrowed to make the first book. And that was not the last of it. She has now brought forth three more, plus a book of my photography and this one of my life. I will always be grateful to her.

One evening in 1985, after 4 ½ years of celibacy, running, preparing myself for the Boston Marathon, me and two of my friends, women bodybuilders, went to a poetry reading of a local

Ann Arbor poet. Because we were late to this poetry reading, we had to sit up front on the floor. When the reading was over, I turned around and I saw these two eyes looking at me, like 'Who the hell is he?' I saw her eyes and I said, 'Who the hell are you? I'd like to know you.' I said that I write poetry as well and that's why I'm here. And she said 'I'm here to meet people.' The thing that attracted me to her was that she's the only woman that did not ask me 'Where are you from?' and 'How long did you have that beard?' I knew then that she was a little bit more than the regular person.

I told her I'd like to see her. She said okay. We made a date. The night before the date, I saw her drinking beer with a tall guy with a bicycle on the street at the Ethnic Festival in Ann Arbor. I said to myself, 'That's not the girl I could make a relationship with.' Since I was not looking for sex, it did not bother me much, so I decided to cancel our date. Well, the next morning, before I could call her, she called me and left a message that she couldn't make the date because she had a concussion. Usually, people just say they have a headache. But a concussion! That did it for me! I understood that she was not interested. Some days went by and she called me again and asked why she hadn't heard from me. I said, 'Normally people say they have a headache. But when someone says they have a concussion, I understand severely. I knew when I was getting the cold shoulder.' She insisted it was true.

At that time, we made another date. It was for Saturday morning. I didn't understand why a date had to be in the morning. We went to this restaurant that she suggested. The waitress told us to follow her to the table. I went to the table, turned around and she wasn't there. I didn't know what was happening to her. Apparently, she knew someone on the way and stopped to visit with them. After some time, I looked around and she saw me waiting. She broke away from that and came to see me. We finished breakfast and she said she had to go to work. That was pretty depressing, especially when I wasn't looking for anything. I did not want to continue this, so I didn't pursue it any further. I didn't call her again. Since I was celibate anyway, I thought I'd let it go.

Then she called me, and I said, 'Now what? What's the next game?' She suggested we get together in the afternoon. I said, 'I can't. I go to Vic Tanny; I run 10 miles.' I would go to Vic Tanny every day after work to run with a group. It so happened she also belonged to Vic Tanny. I was part of an Artists' Group that was musicians, poets and painters, who got together and shared. I told her there was going to be a meeting and if she wanted to come, she could meet me in Vic Tanny, and from Vic Tanny we would go to the meeting. Safety in numbers. But before I went to Vic Tanny, they called the meeting off. So, I ran, and then came to meet her in the jacuzzi. I didn't know what to do. I said, 'I have a problem. The meeting I promised you is not going to be there. I'll give you a few choices: you could go home, or we could go to a restaurant, or we could go to a grocery store, buy some food and we'll go to my place and I'll cook for you.' She agreed to go to the grocery store and then go to my house. And then, as my usual behavior of wanting to make people happy and smile, I saw a young lady at the store was cutting watermelon. I joked with her, made her happy, got a piece of watermelon. Later on, I found out that was the time Judy's heart opened to me. We bought all the fruit and produce that we couldn't identify, to take home. We came home and we both liked what I cooked.

I said, 'Are we going to get together again?' She said, 'I'm going to Hawaii.' I said, 'Well, I'm going to Alaska.' I said, 'When we get back, I'll call you.' So, when I came back, I called her. 'How about next weekend?' 'I'm going to see the Queen.' I began to think that she's no longer normal. I asked her, 'What Queen? I'm going to see the King!' 'The Queen of Serbia.' I was quite secure I wasn't going to lose my virginity. Then she called back and we had dinner together and, after dinner, she wanted to go home. I told her she was secure here, that she could stay. She did. Then we went to bed. Without my permission, she took everything away from me. I remember the next day I was walking with her and she said, 'Why me?' And I said, 'Why not?' But I did not walk with her like she was a girlfriend. I was not used to that. She wanted to hold my hand and walk with me. I was uncomfortable. But she won. She is now the biggest treasure of my life.

[Now, if I may interject. I'm Judy, and I'd like to describe some points of our meeting from my vantage point.

I went to the poetry reading to meet someone. I thought that would be a better way than going to a bar. But I hated poetry. I was introduced to it in high school and never understood it. Hosain, on the other hand, was immersed in beautiful poetry all his life. When I found out about <u>his</u> poetry, it stole my heart. I was so taken by his poetry, I began writing my own!

The day he saw me drinking beer with a man (I'd never seen before or since) at the Ethnic Festival, I had had a new basket hung over the back wheel of my bike. Riding it back home, the basket clipped the fender of a parked car right near my apartment. I was flung over the handlebars and I landed on my head on the street. It was a concussion! I came out of it fine, thanks to my angel brother, Chip.

I was a psychotherapist. When we went to the restaurant and he lost me for a bit, I had run into an ex-client and stopped to talk to her for a few minutes. But I didn't let him know; I just stopped.

The last part was about the Queen. Longtime friends of my brother, Chip, who lives in Ann Arbor, and who were also friends of mine, had amazing dress-up parties in the Chicago area, with unique and delicious food. The couple who put it on was the Queen of Serbia and the Prince Bishop; we all had titles. This was before Serbia became a country. I wasn't kidding. For some reason, outrageous-sounding things happened as we were getting our footing, but it all worked out—and beautifully!]

[Judy again here! We had a six-week pre-wedding honeymoon, where we drove to the Gaspé Peninsula in Canada, which is northeast of Maine. Then we had a normal month-long honeymoon, where we drove to the southwest.]

Judy was 36 when we met and we married just short of her 40th birthday. A decision to have a child would have to have been made right away. Out of love and respect for my wishes, she agreed not to have a child. I'm grateful that she has helped me parent David.

I was asked what advice I have for couples who want to remain in love. Remaining in love is half the story. To be love is the rest of the story. When you are love, it's the easiest way of responding in kind. The more you show it physically, emotionally and are dependent on each other, the stronger the relationship. Try to become a reflection of your spouse, which means you understand her enough to become her or him. It's like osmosis—exchanging love. That makes love grow every day, and there is no reason to stop. Every day is a new day—new love. Just like when you kissed the first time, it is never finished. When you kiss, the work isn't done.

In regard to Judy and I, we have overcome our individuality. No longer on firm grounds, for we have truly become one, knowing how precious life is with loving and being within each other. Home is when Judy and I are together. One of my favorite things is to hold her hand on my face when we're sitting together. It's just like food to your soul. It makes me feel whole again. You keep intimacy alive by letting your heart go free.

My wife's name is Judy. The owner of my heart is Judy. All that I am proud of is Judy. The only companion that stood by me in several incidents of escaping the fangs of death is Judy. The only person who put me together and disciplined me in order to put my four books of poetry together and forced me to sit down and listen to the selections of those poems is Judy. The one who chose the right poems to channel the right projection of my feelings is Judy. The one who fought with me to make my days brilliant and prepared me to read poetry is Judy. So, who is this Judy? Is she someone to sleep with, eat with, argue with, fight for money with, decide who's the boss and who runs this little gathering called marriage? Judy is above all of that. She was there before I asked. She was present when I asked. She never fought back; instead loved me back. In the past, I have given her many names: friend, companion, lover, precious and, of course, in an instant of madness on my part, I have called her unmentionable names. She's a friend so close that at times every move she makes is my move. Sometimes we say things exactly the same at the same time. She has become so close to me, that I cannot separate her from me. In one word, she is me. Judy, I will be with you, even when I'm gone. This love is forever.

My Dear Wife ~

I don't know how I can express
    your devotion
    your love
    your caring
It is priceless

I don't even think the best God in the world
    can express that
Thank you, Beautiful Creature

There is nothing like you in my life
And I am the gladdest to be around you
I love you
    with the deepest love I can muster

And I thank you
    and keep thanking you
        to my last breath
Thank you for being my best friend

Hosain

Hosain

You are a bird
whose sweet song purifies every listening heart

You are the sunrise
whose brilliant colors pull light from darkness

You are the breeze
a gentle hand to lift birds in flight

Keep singing the world into light and flight, Love

Keep singing

Judy

Creator / Inventor

I always tried to make all the things I could—make them better and bigger, rather than buy them. The first time I remember being creative was in Iran when I was in grade school. I was trying to make some kind of a connection with a battery so I could turn lights off and on from a switch under a table. I was successful.

I not only love to teach; I love to learn. I took classes in welding, blacksmithing, woodturning, photography and cooking. Once I was interested in making something, I'd go out and find the best source to learn from.

Photography:

I took workshops with Ansel Adams for three summers. One of the workshops required that I have a view camera. I couldn't afford one, so I made it. I describe this experience, making an enlarger, a developer, a print washer and a darkroom in the Photographer / Traveler chapter.

Music:

I made a dulcimer, sitar, large hand drums, one frame drum 4' in diameter, a steel conga drum, a fiberglass tar, a wooden electric tar, a drum stringer, santur and dombak.

I like amplified guitars, so I made a tar with a pickup so I could amplify it and play the tar like an electric guitar. The tar is the precursor to the guitar and the sitar.

Woodturning:

I made 3 sizes of wood lathes from medium to bigger than I could buy, so I could turn large drums. I made the biggest one so I could turn a 4'-wide frame drum–and I did. And I made a steady rest, which holds the turning to keep the wood from vibrating. I loved making the lathe, then turning the drum on the lathe and then playing the drum.

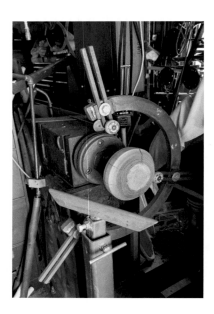

I made my own woodturning tools and chisels. I made the longest goblet [53" tall] and smallest goblet [11¼" tall x less than ½" wide] according to David Ellsworth, the president of the American Woodturners Association. I've also turned all sizes of hand drums and, of course, bowls.

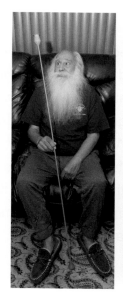

Tools:

I made chisels for blacksmithing. I also learned how to harden the steel so it wouldn't break.

I made a big cubic structure out of steel with two opposite sides as gates that open. Then I can hang the musical instrument and open one side, spray it on one side, close the gate, then open the other side and spray the other side of the instrument. Then I close it so dust will not get in there until it's dry. I used it for musical instruments or any artwork.

In order to bend wood, if you steam the wood in a closed area so the steam stays in there so it penetrates the wood, it becomes soft. You could bend it to any shape you want to. Then use a rope to hold the curves in place until it dries. So, I made a steam wood bender.

I also re-built car engines. I bought a book for dummies before those books were made. It talked about how to re-build an engine. I re-built a VW Bug with an external oil cooler and 4 carburetors instead of one. I also had to create a hoist for the car engine. All of this took a lot of cutting and welding of metal.

RV Camper:

Judy and I loved to travel and photograph, but we needed a vehicle to live in while we traveled. It was too expensive to stay in motels every night and eat every meal in a restaurant. So, I set out to make a camper with a kitchen, a bed and a bathroom. Of course, we needed room for all the photography equipment we would be taking. I got the metal and wooden frame finished, the walls of the bathroom and some of the kitchen. We live right next to the expressway, so I decided to take it for a test drive. I backed our pickup to it and was able to place the camper on it and secure it in place. We drove it a mile or two up the highway and it felt so top heavy, I had to carefully turn around. Needless to say, I gave up on that idea. It remains in the back yard to this day as a storage camper. We eventually bought a proper camper.

Persian Bidet:

Moslems must wash after using the bathroom. I created a certain plumbing that produces water in the location where it's needed, directed by one's hand holding a hose that can easily be turned on and off. This apparatus is secured to the wall next to the toilet for easy use.

Chef:

I made a pig roaster. In it, we cooked a 230# pig. I also made a grill with a hood, as well as a cast iron table that stands over an open fire, so you can sit around it and cook things. I bought an old freezer for $75 and, with the help of a friend, made it into a smoker that holds 90# of meat. And I made a meat pounder (or gooshkoob in Farsi) made out of wood.

I had an Asian rice cooker. That kind of cooker keeps rice warm for a few days, so it's ready to eat at any time, although I'm sure it doesn't last that long in an Asian household. Persian rice cookers make golden crusts on the bottom, so when you turn it over to serve it on a platter, it's beautiful and crispy and inviting. I jerry rigged my rice cooker to change its nationality from Asian to Persian.

Kolbeh:

We used to go to the ocean and go into the water and come out and enjoy ourselves. Judy found out she was sensitive to the sun. She got skin cancer on her arms. So, we didn't go to the oceans. We made a gathering place in the back yard out of plastic tubing with a tarp over the top. On a windy day, we lost it. I built one with metal tubing. A stronger wind came, and blew that one down, too. I decided I had enough of that, so I built our current 24' x 30' structure with 5½"x 5½" wolmanized posts and invited the Woodturners Club to one of my tastiest BBQs. Before they came, I had bought all the trusses. And when they came, I said they had to put the roof up. And David and Judy shingled the roof. The first roof made the smoke billow all around. So, I created a second roof along the peak length with open sides, called a ridge vent, so the smoke could go out. Judy made that roof vent. (I'm scared of heights.) We had to get a building permit for the Kolbeh.

In Farsi, Kolbeh means "spiritual nest." We use this structure in our back yard to grill and smoke food for gatherings of friends and family. It's like a gazebo. In the center is a fire pit. I made it from a used tractor rim for $20. The center of the pit is equipped with an oxygenator–a mechanism I made from a gas forge to continually pump oxygen into the bottom of the fire so there's less smoke. Above the fire, I installed an overhead hook with a pulley for pots.

Since the time of its construction, we've had many joyful gatherings. Our good friend, Mark, put in a sound system so we can have mics for music and speaking. He also put in beautiful colored lights and a handy electric outlet over the serving table for coffee machines, pot warmers, etc. that stores in the rafters. I call people to eat with an old, rusty, steel bell I made from an oxygen tank, which rings with the swing of a wooden mallet, which I also made. I've had the best possible gatherings there that you could imagine.

Sauna:

Early on, I built a wooden sauna in my basement. In the winter, friends would come over and we'd take our clothes off, go outside and roll around in the snow. Then we'd come back inside to the warmth of the sauna. It was refreshing.

Fertility Optimizer:

Many years ago, I also invented a tool to measure uterus contractions. There was a doctor who was specializing in infertility at U of M Hospitals. I worked with him with women who couldn't get pregnant, trying to find the optimal time when a woman could become pregnant. He wanted to know about the contractions of the uterus, because that's one of the elements that sucks in the semen. This determines whether a woman gets pregnant. I made an instrument with a balloon at the end with an anchor outside of the uterus, so the instrument will go into the uterus and the anchor will be on the outside of the uterus, like a fish hook, so the instrument would not come out of the uterus. It was called an 'anchor.' Then I put water in it, so it would touch all parts of the uterus. And I made an electronic measuring instrument that would show the pressure in the uterus–the uterus changes. Some are naturally inclined to be a fertile environment. We measured uterus contractions in order to find out what kind of contractions produce pregnancy. This test was done before, during and after the premenstrual cycle. We also had the woman read about sexual activities or look at them and then we'd measure the contractions and whether or not they changed. There was a textbook for their medical school published on our work.

My mind is always in a creative mode. If I see a wood lathe, I see that the size I want isn't there, so I'd have to make it. I use my imagination and problem solving and my physics background. When I see something that I like, I try to see if I can make it better.

Photographer / Traveler

In high school in Iran, I was a lifeguard near the Caspian Sea. I met a man who was photographing the sunrise with a view camera. We talked. I went to his shop. He showed me how to retouch negatives. I was hooked.

At that time, across from the school was a Singer Sewing Machine store, where they sold the machine and taught people how to use it. There was one beautiful girl who would come to learn how to sew with two other girls. I fell in love with her. Not being able to talk to her, as was the custom at the time, I walked behind her and said funny things, so she would laugh and it would make me very happy. And then I was coming to America, wanting to have an image of her. I purchased a Minox camera, which was very small and used as a spy camera. I would go in front of her while she was walking, turn around and photograph her. Later on, I found out she was a friend of Badri, my cousin. So, she invited her to a party. I was able to dance with her. I also took a lot of photographs of my country. Then I came to America with the same camera. Since I was lonely and interested in finding friends, I kept taking their pictures and showing them to them. I also showed them places I had visited in America as well as my culture and where I was born. That was 1955. I kept photographing to the present day.

I love to travel. The day after school let out, I'd pack up and go traveling with my cameras.

I started photographing with the Minox camera, which has a thumbnail-sized negative. Then I bought a Leica M3 and three lenses and joined the Ann Arbor Camera Club in the early 60s. I met Howard Bond and saw his beautiful photographs, which were at that time from an 11"x 14" view camera. Then I decided to learn from him. He was very gracious, helped me in any way he could. He talked about an Ansel Adams workshop that he had attended at Yosemite. I had one problem. I did not have a view camera, which was necessary to attend Ansel Adams' workshop. It cost $1000, which I couldn't afford.

A professor at the U of M School of Architecture, named Les Fader, was teaching his students how to make a 4"x 5" camera for architectural photography. I went to him, asked him if I could attend his class, but I wanted to make an 8"x 10" view camera rather than 4"x 5". He asked me if I was familiar with woodworking machines. I said I was. He agreed to help me build an 8"x 10" camera with the agreement that his time was for his 4"x 5" students, and I assured him that I would require very little of his time. I scaled everything from 4"x 5" to 8"x 10". So, I made one for $100, which had a 40" long bellows and unlimited movement on the front standard and back standard, which was much more flexible than the commercial ones. I made the camera body with plywood and I ordered a bellows from New York. I still have this camera.

Then I attended the Zone System workshop in Yosemite with Ansel Adams. There were 20 people there for a week. It was maybe $400 for a workshop in the mid 70s. When he saw my camera, he said, 'What the hell is that?' He was very impressed with my camera. He asked me if he could use it. I was more than happy to step aside and have him compose and take a picture with my camera. In this workshop, I met many great photographers. Among them were Morley Baer (some of his photographs were better than Ansel's), Paul Caponigro, Allen Ross, who was Adams' assistant, and John Sexton, who was carrying Adam's camera and tri-pod, setting up for his demonstrations.

One day, I was assigned to work with Morley Baer to photograph with him and learn from him. I praised him for his knowledge of taking photographs and developing them in the old-fashioned chemistry. It was a pleasure to work with him. He also showed interest in my camera. At night when we all got together, we discussed photography. I listened to him very carefully and learned about his chemistry about photography. Later on, I took a workshop with him and John Sexton.

In the workshop I took with Ansel Adams, I saw some of the things that were done. I saw the formula that Edward Weston sent to his son in the war, directing his son how to be sure to get his negative properly developed. I was able to get a copy of the formula—actually, a copy of his letter to his son, who is Brett Weston. From that formula, which had different chemicals mixed together to make the developer, I spent about seven years to develop my own by adding and subtracting different chemicals and seeing the result—and not poisonous chemicals. Out of that, I created a developer, which would not go bad for a long time. It didn't oxidize as much as others.

There was the Victor School of Photography in Victor, CO. I went there to visit. I shared my formula with Al Weber. He was the owner and director of this school and was a professor of photography at the University of California. I did a small workshop there to teach about my developer. He liked it. He asked me to come back the next summer. I did that three times and each time I also spent time with Ansel Adams attending his workshops.

The Zone System is a system for photographers to make sure that a negative is completely developed, so textures are continuous from the darkest to the brightest. This was Ansel's major contribution to the photography world.

I visited Ansel Adams in his darkroom and saw his most famous image 'Moon Over Hernandez.' I was very much interested in enlarging 8"x 10" negatives. When I got home, I invented an enlarger for 8"x 10" negatives out of an old 5"x 7" enlarger. I also had an old 4"x 5" enlarger. I invented a head, which would take an 8"x 10" negative instead of a 4"x 5" one. I also converted a 4"x 5" enlarger to a 5"x 7" one. I made an enlarger box to accommodate the necessary height for the placement of the light for an 8"x 10" negative rather than a 4"x 5". I successfully made photographs, with two different light sources to control the contrast, which is called a variable contrast enlarger.

I invented the two lights by going to a sign maker. I told him the two colors and gave him the wavelength of the two colors to control the contrast. I also made 10,000 watts of power. The sign maker made it possible for me to control the contrast. I made a formula that would tell me, by reading the negative contrast out of that, that I could control the two colors in the enlarger. So, when I got to the enlarger, I had known the contrast in the negative, then adjusted the two lights in the enlarger, and achieved a full range of shades of gray in the print.

I did not wish to copy what Ansel Adams and those other great photographers were doing, but I watched them, learned from what they were doing. Doing that, I found my own way of photography with their influence. I think that Ansel Adams would have embraced digital photography.

I built my own darkroom in my basement in 1975. Because I was claustrophobic, I needed open air. But also, the light couldn't come in. Therefore, I made two U-shaped walls to form an S-shape for the entrance to it, and painted it black. It wouldn't allow light to come into the darkroom. I made a large sink to do all the processing. It was large enough to hold four trays, which were for soaking the print, then developing it, then stopping the developing and washing it. I had a chair that I could roll around in order to be accessible to the four trays. I also made an adjacent second room for my 5"x 7" enlarger.

I also built a print washer, which was divided into ten different spaces. When I put the print in it, I slid the print vertically and put it in the print washer, so that the prints didn't stick together and so it thoroughly washed all the chemicals out of it.

I built a truck camper to travel and photograph in, but unfortunately that was a flop. I made it out of angle irons and particleboard. With all the walls, except the back one, and ceiling in place and the fridge and toilet stall mounted, I drove down the expressway next to my home and found it was way too top heavy. It was unusable for travel, so it became a storage unit in our back yard. For traveling, I bought a cargo van. I converted the back of the van to a dark area to be able to change negatives.

Ansel photographed Canyon de Chelly in northeastern Arizona. It inspired me to want to photograph it myself. I didn't want to take the same photograph Ansel did, so I chose another angle, plus it was winter. There was a small river that was iced over between Canyon de Chelly and me. I asked an Indian where else to cross. I had 80 pounds of backpack. As I walked across, the ice broke. I jumped to the next piece of ice. I twisted my neck. I took the photograph, finished up my trip and drove home to Michigan. I went back to teach school for three days. The fourth day I couldn't move my neck. I went to ER. I was in traction for three months. Luckily, I've had no lasting problems from that time. As it turns out, I think the photograph I took was better than Ansel's.

During this time, I began to write poetry. I played music and I photographed extensively, traveling wherever it was possible and photographing as many places as I could physically go to. And all winter I developed and printed those images. I started with a Minox camera, to a 35 mm camera, to an 8"x 10" View Camera, back down to 5"x 7", because I couldn't carry that much weight any longer. And now I am totally digital.

In the 60s I wanted to go to Mexico to photograph. I got to the border. I had a beard. They wouldn't let me over the border until I cut my beard. I refused to do that, so I turned around, passing the American Consulate. They didn't stop me or ask me questions when I went by; they just smiled. They knew I'd be turned away. Haven't cut it since.

One year I was photographing Big Bend, TX. After photographing all day, I went to a hot springs there. The people were all naked. I got in. After awhile they left. I saw some kids. My butt was burning from some sand that got in it. At night, I wanted to put some Betadine on my crack to dry it up. So, I got in my little VW and tried to bend around to do this. I accidently opened the car door and the lights went on. Embarrassed, I got in my car and drove away to another campsite.

In 1979, I was visiting Fayette, MI, a ghost town in the Upper Peninsula. I was walking behind the group with a guide and I overheard him say it was his last year of being a guide at Fayette, meaning they would be closing Fayette. I photographed the area. I took the photographs and asked my dear friend, Pete, to write a poem for each one. Then I asked to see Senator Faust in Lansing, MI, the capital. He said Fayette would be abandoned. I wanted them to see what they were abandoning. I told them passionately that this is what they're going to destroy. They listened to me. I mounted the photographs and gave them to the Michigan Historical Museum in Lansing. They took the photographs and added them to a collection they had for saving places in Michigan. They asked me for the right of using the photographs for the purpose of having people come to see the site. I gave them permission to publish my work. They went through their governmental processes and two years later they published the magazine with my photographs in it. When I went to revisit Fayette a couple years later, there was a new Visitor's Center, which they didn't have before. It became a part of Michigan's official ghost towns and could no longer be destroyed. I felt good about being an integral part of keeping it alive. A lot of its buildings have been preserved. It's a beautiful place to visit.

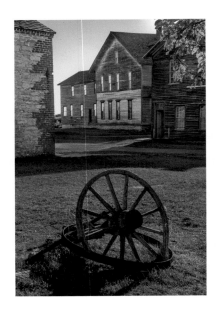

Dear Pete was also an integral part of another endeavor in 1981. I picked out 30 of my black and white photographs from Canada, the United States and Scotland and convinced Pete to write poetry to them. He was so inspired that he, his wife and I spent the weekend together and he completed his task. The following weekend, a musician friend of ours, John, heard the poetry and saw the photographs and immediately began composing music for specific ones. Together, the three of us formed Troika Image Arts, Inc., and performed together at a number of locations and venues including: Michigan Council for the Arts, a private showing in Detroit, Detroit Sierra Club Spring Fundraiser and the Sierra Club Annual Banquet, a Wayne State University Environmental Club on Belle Isle and a number of local libraries. Eventually, John selected seven of the original pieces to produce a fine CD entitled 'Caress of Change.'

I retired in 1993 and Judy continued to work. It was during this time that I worked on developing my photography and other creations. But I wanted to travel and photograph and didn't want to do it alone. So, I convinced Judy to retire in 2000 so we could travel together. Judy carried my tripod, then carried my camera, then complained, then convinced me that I should reduce the size of my camera equipment to match my age and my physical ability. And now she carries her own digital camera, her own tripod, and stands in front of my camera to take her own pictures. What a joy to see her development.

I've taken Judy to Iran twice, Germany, China, India, Turkey, and all states and Canada many times. I've taken over 30,000 images of Iran and have shown them to clubs, family and friends, and to fund-raising events for a good cause. Before I knew Judy, I went to Scotland with Howard Bond. I also photographed Alaska three times.

Nature is my greatest teacher. I used to go to the big trees in the Redwood Forest, walk around. If there was no one around, I'd hug the trees. Nowadays, I invite them to hug the trees and be grateful for their existence. If I was a tree, I'd be a cherry tree. I love cherries. Cherry blossoms are colorful, have a lovely fragrance and are delicious—in other words, they are beautiful. And when the cherries become fully grown, they appear like jewels.

I was asked if I could travel anywhere in the world today, where would I go. Shiraz. It's my source of my creativity. That's the way people are there. It's like going to the top of a mountain, seeing what you've gotten from that—your energy, vision and inspiration.

When I first witnessed the digital world, I fell in love out of necessity for its lightness and portability, which saved Judy from being my private sherpa, and which, once again, got us on the road. Nowadays, with the extensive advance of digital cameras and inkjet printers, I am in heaven. I think digital can actually do better than any film photography.

For this belief, I was almost thrown out of our Camera Club. But I persevered.

I brought back to life the digital photography club at Washtenaw Community College and named it 'Digitizers.'

And about a photography book, forget it. What I have put Judy through with even the first poetry book, if I mention a book of photography, she would surely put me in the doghouse, and that is not where I want to be. It's too cold in the winter, and not photogenic in the summer.

But then a dear friend of ours, Dan, who also worked with Ansel Adams and lived with him for 6 months, volunteered to put together a book of my photography and some poetry. Thank goodness for online publishing, which can do an excellent job. It's called 'Hosain's Vision.'

https://www.blurb.com/b/9780935-hosain-s-vision

I have exhibited my photography in several places: The Art Institute of Chicago, the Pierce Street Gallery in Birmingham, MI, The Camera Obscura Gallery in Denver, CO, Soho Gallery in New

York City, NY and the Photography Exhibit of Fayette Historical Ghost Town in Fayette, MI. My permanent collections are in the following institutions: Art Institute of Chicago, University of Michigan Art Museum, Michigan Historical Museum in Lansing, MI, Victor School of Photography in Victor, CO, the Detroit office of the Smithsonian Institute, Penkill Castle, Scotland and a studio in Düsseldorf, Germany.

Friend

Close your eyes. Put away everything. Your world becomes very, very lonely. Friends come in many colors, religions and all that goes with it and all shades of gray. Everything I have learned came from friends. And everything I have passed on to friends came from friends. So, as a friend, I have been carrying the love I have received and shared it. That makes friendship much closer. I wouldn't be where I am without friends. It would be like speaking in a vacuum—no one to share with, no one to love, no one to care for. I expect I would be a very, very lonely person without friends. I get hugs from friends and the hugs stay with me for a long time. When you hold someone close enough, there is an exchange that is not visible, but can be felt. Like a dog, once they see you, smell you, they will remember you. I say 'Good Morning' to every friend. I never want the day to go down in darkness. There is always one sad thing about friendships: when they are gone, a piece of me goes with them. I make friends with children who understand me more than their parents. My best poems are written for children. They're pure, believable and could respond as well. I have acquired a few children who are poets, writers and lifetime friends. If you could tell me how you could live without friends, I would like to know about it. Keeping friends is a big job. But loving friends secures them for a lifetime—and that is what I live for. Sometimes I see a person; I don't know them, but I love them. Can you imagine how your life would be if you always walked among friends? That is the meaning of my life: my friends.

For a long time, we had an answering machine message that I put on our phone:

> Hosain is the name
> Friendship is my game
> Love to hear your heart
> Will return your call on my next breath

Friendship is being present, being loving. In times of need, you don't have to ask for help. They will be there before you need them. Here's a poem I wrote about friendship:

When you are sad
    I run to the garden
    to gather flowers
    to brighten your heart

When you are happy
    I run to your arms
    for a dance

And when you are crying
    I gather the tears
    to grow sweet fruit trees

When you are limping
    I am your cane
I will catch you if you fall

In other words
    I will be there before you need me

If you're able to be a friend to yourself, then it is easy to be a friend to others. The need to be friends is visible. In other words, I've got your back.

I have an unknown friend named Babak. We met at Shabe Shehr–Persian Poetry Night. I was reading poetry. Afterwards, he yelled from the back, 'We have the same heart!' It was Babak and Ginger who helped us gather my life for this book.

One time I was asked to show my photographs. I told them I was unable to do that, because to do that I needed to frame them. I was not able financially to do that. Babak suggested that the cost should be taken up by the Iranian members. It was an exhibit about Iran. He asked me how much it cost. I told him $2500 with that many frames. A few days later, he wrote me a check for $2500, and he secured our friendship for life. He demonstrated his heart was open. I have many friends like that.

Another sweet friend is Jim. When I was sick in the hospital for two weeks, he stayed with me every other night all night long, even though I was not aware of it. He comes and cuts the grass, cuts the trees, fixes things around my house, makes fires, and once a month, in memory of our hospital experience, we spend an all-nighter. We cook, we eat, we watch TV and spend most of the night the way we used to be together in the hospital. The other nights at the hospital, my neighbor, dear Cheryl, stayed with me all night long, watching over me. It feels great that so many people I love, love me back. And, of course, I have many, many friends who care, and, fortunately, not just for me, but for everyone around us. And every time we gather for any occasion, we spend all night by the fire–jokes, wine, just practicing togetherness. Can't imagine it could get any better than that.

Yesterday I came home
Guess what was there?
Many cards and roses
    that brought me back to life

I never knew I was so important in anyone's life
But now I know
Friends are for life
And life itself is a friend
Treat it that way

Judy, my wife, is my best friend. She is with me, even when I am not with her. We start the day with sitting on the couch and she lays on my chest. After breakfast, she puts her head on my lap and I rub her shoulder while we watch TV. At night, when we go to bed, she spoons with me and puts her hand on my chest, and I feel the best in my life. Is there a need to say anymore?

I got double pneumonia twice, ready to die. On one occasion, a priest came to give me my last rights and Judy told him not to go in because it would upset me. Then I had double pneumonia again. This time they brought a dog for me to pet. So, I lost a priest, but I gained the friendship of a dog. Every time I opened my eyes into consciousness, Judy was next to me holding my hand.

Sun, moon and me . . . three friends
At night
    moon shines my heart
Daytime
    sun warms my soul
And I
    in days or nights
        offer my adoration and absolute obedience

Isn't this what friendship means?

We are all one family, many hearts beating in harmony, and the goal is to strive to make humanity one concert, and everyone is in harmony and no one will be left behind and lonely.

Poet

My grandmother passed in away in 1956, after I moved to America. I was the only one that was not at her bedside. She asked my mother to give her a picture of me. She held it and then passed away. When I received this news, I was so hurt because at that time I was married with a son and she didn't even know it, because my father was against marriage with someone other than Moslem. I was so moved, my whole life changed. I had no one to cry with, no one to talk to. Alone in my dorm, I sat down and wrote a very angry letter to my mother and father. I expressed my anger, told them that my grandmother, who I most loved, missed knowing that I had a son. While I was writing this letter, I was crying and the tears fell on the paper. I didn't bother to rewrite it. I just mailed it that way. My father did not respond, but my mother did. She mentioned how beautifully I expressed my anger. She told me, 'This is not a letter, this is a poem–like all the ones I used to read to you from Hafez.' As usual, she influenced me again to write and express in the deepest way I can. She was herself a poet. That was my first strike at writing poetry.

When I came to this country, I had lost many friends of mine in the Revolution. I did not speak English. As a result, I did not have many friends. Going to school was my only contact with people. When I would get back to my dorm room and finish my homework, I would cry of loneliness. I remember once I wrote a letter to my Father, and when I finished it, some of the words on the paper were smeared. I realized it was my fallen tears. No one could understand my tears better than I. So, I began to write extensive letters of feelings to the friends and family I left behind. And when I learned English well enough and had left everything behind so I could survive in this country, I had a lot to say. So, I began to write poetry in English, however the language was limiting to me. But I was able to relay the feelings. After two broken marriages, a son that I abandoned and a few broken relationships, I began to write emotional poetry. And when I shared it with friends, they encouraged me to write a book—write more and share more. Although I had everything I needed to continue, I needed these friends to keep me going, to light my fire, and let me burn in love instead of anger and loneliness.

Some trails I have traveled
were never level
Some trails were level
and always shining
And some trails
rainy and muddy
all day, every day

But this is the only way to learn
how to travel
alongside wisdom

I was asked why I choose to express my thoughts and feelings in poems rather than in essays. I didn't understand the question. When you have to say something and not knowing how to say it, you write an essay. A poem is short verses that say what you think, what you feel, without explanation. In other words, short words and infinite amount of meanings, like a jewel box rather than a library.

Poetry is more important for me than photography. In photography, I could capture an instantaneous feeling with the use of acquired equipment, and it was limited only to summer vacation and the ability to acquire the equipment. But in poetry, I was able to write poetry in the classroom when the students were taking tests or at home watching TV or reading a book or listening to music. Or I could spend 100% facing my heart and writing down my feelings. It was a great satisfaction. It brought me a lot of peace and stability. I would like to shine a light on every heart so that they could feel what they see and respond more to the hearts than to the mind. More care and love come from the speaking heart, and less harm comes from people who follow their hearts. If I can do that much, I have served my fellow people the best I could. A shining heart is the solution to our problems. Photography was my second important work because it was similar. For example, I traveled to Alaska three times to get a clear shot of Mount McKinley–a 12,000-mile trip. My photographs were an expression of poetry.

Sometimes I had a feeling, but couldn't bring it into words, slept on it and dreamt about a poem and completed it in my dreams. It was absolutely timeless, placeless and free that I could even write it in my dreams. And sometimes, when I was writing, I would write, unconsciously, poems that became my best.

Poetry is the next best thing to breathing. Breathing is an exercise to keep me alive. Poetry is the instrument that sent me free and shined a light in my heart for the way to love freely and unconsciously. It was like I was riding on clouds, raining poetry and feeding the roses. I think you would feel the same if you stopped thinking and started feeling. Writing poetry comes freely to me with no thought. Sometimes, if I need to open to it, I read Hafez–and then I burst out and become free.

Persians love poetry. We have had many poets through the ages. Rumi, Hafez and Saadi are well known throughout the world. Rumi, whose poetry my mother sang to me as a child, has been the best-selling poet in America for some years now, and he lived 800 years ago. It is said that anyone who was born in Shiraz, Iran is a poet. Hafez and Saadi were born in Shiraz. That's where I was born. That's what I was sentenced to. And so far, I have written around 26,000 poems. There is no difference between Sufi poetry and Islamic poetry.

I have enjoyed sharing my poetry in many different settings. I've also taught others, in workshops, how to create their own poetry. It's sculpting love into poetry. Poetry is my most significant contribution. And my most rewarding moment as a poet is when I know someone understood me.

With the love and support of my wife, Judy, I have written four books of poetry. Each poem in my books is an image of a living moment in my life. Life as you live it has infinite phrases, poetry, music, colors, songs, sadness, happiness, births and deaths. And a book of life has infinite chapters and a complete universe of feelings. I have no regrets, only great hope for our family of mankind.

www.AWinkForYourHeart.com

I am sharing these poems to invite you into my heart. Then you can send yourself free. Like when you taste a drop of the ocean, you taste the whole ocean. Or when you fall in love, you are free. The center of interest will move from you to the Beloved, therefore you are unlimited. You've got to be so open without barrier, that others join you without limits and feel welcome. The time for blending is the time for loving. Blending means no barriers. I am so in love with loving that I see love everywhere—trees, dogs, alligators, birds and all the rest. I see the whole creation from the point of loving it. I don't think I would be alive without love. Going through life, no matter how difficult it was, love carried me through. When you stand for love, there is no separation between you and the whole of creation. And the cosmos is your home.

You taste one drop of an ocean
    you know the taste of the whole ocean

You taste a kiss from one lover
    you surrender to love your whole life

You see one sunset
    you fall in love with colors forever

On a starry night with full shining moon
    you become a part of the universe for eternity

Like two candles
    rushing to make the same flame

Like the ocean waves
    rushing to meet the shores

Like waterfalls free-falling
    to resemble the naked power of beauty

Like a songbird saying
    'I am singing my heart out for you'

Like night
    rushing to meet the sun
        to give birth to a new day

Tell me
Is this not a tapestry of love
    which is our home?

Let us pour our hearts into a keg
Where we can blend with each other
    to brew wine
    and to make a general amnesty
        to all who get intoxicated with this wine

What harm would it do
    if a drunken heart takes over the world
        and says 'You're all free'

Everyone should drink from the same keg
    to become bewildered in love

Follow no direction except
    the oneness
        that tastes no taste but love

Let us brew such wine
    by standing for peace
    and saying 'I love you'
And together saying 'We love us'

Before love
	I did not know who I was

After love
	I did not care who I was

Spring will come again
Blossoms everywhere
	saying hello to the world

We will also blossom

This is the cycle of life
	with one exception:
When love catches up with you
	that blossom will never end

Like a flute
    how can I sing
        without the touch of your lips

Like a flute
    I am lifeless
        without your breath blowing through me

Like a flute
    how can I change my tune
        without the caressing of your fingers

Like love
    how can I exist
        without dissolving in you

Speak
    poetry

Laugh
    from where joy is made

Cry
    as though pearls are rolling off your face

Be sad
    only if you didn't love enough

Speak to me from the heart
How else can I get close to you?

Sing me songs from faraway distances
  so I could travel with peace and understanding
Touch me like you touch a musical instrument
  so I could be in tune with the music of life
Bring me wine made out of tears
  so I could taste the loneliness
   of the ones left behind
Finally
Bring me a rose
  so I could have a companion
   to speak freely with

Love comes first
Without it
    peace will never be achieved

Love comes first
Without it
    the family of man will become extinct

Love comes first
Without it
    no hope can exist

Love comes first
That is why you and I are friends

We need no more than that
Everything else will fall in line
    and is possible
And no hate will ever take its hold
    on any loving heart

Live to be that

Sufi

Sufism is not about me
    nor about you
It's about the harmony we can create
    within humankind

It definitely is not about religion
It's not about faith or belief
It is about a rose
No matter from what angle of life you look
    that rose feels beautiful

People want to know what a Sufi is
My answer is:
    It is not about what is
    It is about what isn't

No, I'm not crazy
Everyone knows that what is
    defines touch, taste, color, heat, sound and the like
And in this world
    we have a finite amount of what is
        which we call 'known'

This universe

    in which we are a miniscule part

      is unknowable

That is where a Sufi wants to dwell

That is what a Sufi needs to know

I hope you reach a higher consciousness

    than you are today

      and never look down

        on the ones who need a rising hand

About my religion, I was raised as a Moslem and witnessed a few Sufis around my Father. I believe my Mother was a Sufi, but I didn't know it. As I learned more and more about religions in general, what people stood for and what they were against, they did not make any godly sense to me. So, I began to free myself from beliefs and naturally fell into Sufism. Sufis have no religion. They accept all religions, at the same time reject all of them. Religions normally put differences between people. Sufis see no differences. We claim we accept everyone, we love everyone and we share with everyone. Religions are not the same.

Sufism started in Iran. Moslems were there. In order to survive, we claimed Moslemhood. We did not wish to be discriminated against. Wherever we are, we need to be accepted as part of their community. How else can Sufis claim 'I am you. You are me. Even though I don't know you, I love you.'

We believe in roses. In fact, the symbol of Sufism is a red rose. It's a beautiful flower, which can be offered to anyone of any age, any religion. How can anyone reach out to you and say 'I love you' and meet resistance? The real Sufis are not visible, for they appear in the hearts of people and need not to be noticed. Anyone can be a Sufi. When you ask questions and listen carefully, receive and give openly, in other words, loving unlimited, you are a Sufi.

Sufis believe either I am nothing or I am everything. I'm not a Jew nor a Moslem nor a Christian. I'm not a Hindu, Buddhist nor a Zoroastrian. Therefore, I make no distinction between them, and I accept them all at once. That makes me everything. Therefore, I am a Jew, a Moslem and a Christian, and every other belief that exists. Yet I do not exist as any of them. I am an image of the creation with one heart. And within that one heart exists a universal love.

I have come from you
for we are born within each other
This poetry is written
about merging in the end
All that separates us is artificial

Just like looking at a rose:
Every eye
no matter what color, race, creed or religion
whether poor, rich, Pope or Prophet
will see the same beauty and intensity in that rose

And to me
that rose is the source of our lives
That is what brings us together
That is where we come from
and that is where we go to

Let us realize that rose for each other

Back in the 1980s, I went to Iran. I wanted to meet a darvish. I searched to find a darvish; no one was to be found. I went to Davoud Mosque. One of the Moslem saints was buried there. We went into the mosque, walked around, kissed the posts around the grave—did the usual things people do when they go into a mosque, which was how to respect the Imam. When we were done, we walked out the door. There was a Darvish right in front of me. I knew he was a Darvish because of certain clothes and hat he wore—pretty ragged. I said I was very happy to see him. I'd been looking for a Darvish. His first words to me were 'It's all about love.' I invited him to come with us to have breakfast, since it was early in the morning. We talked. I asked the meaning of the symbols of the things they carry around. Everyone gathered around us. And I heard someone say, 'What kind of a Darvish are you who doesn't know what these things mean?' I understood that I was supposed to act like a Darvish, so I didn't ask any more questions. For many years I tried to disprove that it was all about love. But life taught me that he was right and I was wrong.

Many years ago, probably in the 1990s, Pir Vlayat Inayat Khan came to Chicago. He was the son of Pir Hazrat Inayat Khan, who brought Sufism to America. Judy's father was the one who told us about this event, so we went. After the gathering, I asked one of the attendees to ask Pir Vlayat Khan to initiate me to become a Sufi. I wanted a piece of everything. He said he doesn't do initiations anymore, but someone else would be happy to do it. After the lecture, I happened to be near him and I asked him if he would initiate me. His response was, 'I would be happy to do that.' He took me to a private room and we had a conversation. He asked me to repeat some things after him. It only took a few minutes, and it was done. Then I asked him why, when he addressed the group, was he talking so technically and trying to prove what Sufism is. He asked me where I was from. I said 'I'm from Iran, where Sufism began.' He told me that Western society needs proof and to be given facts; they're unable to share spiritual feelings without facts. I know that in Iran, the gatherings are meant to share poetry, music and dancing. It becomes a hypnotic state. During the dance, the participants dance until they fall into a trance and sometimes fall to the ground. They are called 'darvishes.' I agreed with his explanation of the difference in the Western world. Either way, when I looked at the people in the audience, I saw peace, kindness and togetherness. There was a buffet. And after everyone brought their food to the tables, they discussed the event in such a way that it was quite obvious it was one family. I loved being among them. I longed to be a part of them. And that's the reason I asked to be initiated.

When love whispers your name
    and flowers send you fragrances

When spring water soothes your pain
    and morning dew cleanses your soul

You are living a life of a Darvish

A Darvish is a soul
    who is invisible to all eyes
    yet present to all hearts

You cannot shackle him
    imprison him
    or starve him

He is above all limitations
    that manhood can put upon him
Yet he is an unlimited lover
    and ultimate true friend

And above all
He believes in you
    and you don't even know it

Meditation is a condition to quiet yourself. Sufis don't do that. They want to yell and scream and share and dance. And lose themselves.

The first time Rumi, the great Persian poet, met his master, Shams-e Tabriz, Shams was listening to Rumi lecturing in a mosque. He questioned him about why he was saying what he was saying. Rumi said, "You don't understand this." Shams threw the book Rumi was reading from into the pool in the mosque. When he pulled it out of the water, it was dry. Rumi asked, "How did you do that?" Shams said, "That's something you don't understand."

When they had been together for about three months, as soon as they would meet together in a Kolbeh (which in Farsi means 'Spiritual Nest'), they would blend with each other. When they were in the Kolbeh for about a month, Rumi came out and twirled around the posts from happiness. This became known as Whirling Dervishes (Turkey) or Whirling Darvishes (Iran). Rumi's sons and students were jealous, so Shams was forced to leave him.

I've been asked how someone who wants to study with someone would find that person. I say know yourself first. Know the feeling inside you. When you face it with love, you understand it. How can anyone teach you the relationship between you and your dog? When you love the dog, something happens to you. It's a relationship that binds you together for life. Unfortunately, the dog dies. Find someone to love. You need to know how it feels to love. That's the opening of your heart.

1. Forgive yourself. It will release you from fear.

2. Love comes to you; don't try to go and find it. Just like a bee finding the flower for the honey. The flower doesn't go to find the bee. They exist because of each other. When the bee sits on the flower, it pollinates it. The bee gets the honey and they cannot live without each other. The killer bees were from Mexico. They were angry. They would swarm and attack people and animals. People realized they didn't want to kill the bees because if they did, plants wouldn't exist. Ultimately, people wouldn't exist. From a single bee, all else exists. Everything is related to everything else.

I saw the Divine in the face of a dog. Any instances that make you realize a sense of responsibility and sacrifice and acceptance and caring is Divine. That's why I always advise people: find something or someone to love; that is the beginning of Divinehood—always there, always grateful, always by your side. What is more Divine than that?

I will never find God, nor do I wish to. What would happen to my life if I found God? There would be no reason to live. So, I keep looking for God in every corner of my life.

Sufism is mostly philosophy and teaching. Sufis literally run with love and make sure no one is without love.

Darvish is a person with a certain quality that is projected without words.

Dervish is Turkish. Darvish is Persian.

A Darvish is basically anyone who has dedicated his/her life to the path of seeking the truth. A Darvish is a person who does not exist, which means his being does not count. His whole existence is to love, to care and to be there. If I exist and you exist, then we are different and create separation. I am me and you're you. But if I don't exist, that means that it is you that is important and who I care for.

A Sufi can be a professor, a preacher. A Darvish devotes everything to love and healing. Some of those are not put in words. Some ways a darvish teaches is by telling stories and by being an example. Mostly, they are musicians, poets, mathematicians and, of course, they are dancers. They have a certain way of singing their poems. It's called 'masnavi.'

A Sufi can teach how to be a Darvish, but cannot be a darvish. In order for you to be teaching, you're transferring things into words to make someone understand. The Darvish understands and makes the people feel themselves. A Darvish can light a candle so people see themselves.

A Sufi is a person who is able to see a loving heart and bring it out in the open to expose its beauty. If you have a heart, you're already a Sufi. Bring it out and share it. The hidden jewel, which is your heart, is within you from the day you're born to the day you're gone. The capacity to be a Sufi is your instinct. Listen to it and you will know the way. Being a Sufi enhances all that you do, because you're supporting everyone who's near you. It goes like this: someone lights a candle and everyone can see the light. Once a Sufi, always a Sufi? Yes. How can you forget the warmth in your heart and not see the flame, which is warming your whole future? Every time you reach out for someone, listen to someone, pet a dog or a cat, listen to frogs at night and birds in the early morning, watch a sunrise or sunset, these are friends reminding you of nature and its beauty and its offering. Take a bite out of a ripe peach, you taste nature and its immense creativity, realizing that one seed grows into a tree and every year gives you fruits. That is nature loving you. If you are in touch with that process, you are a Sufi. In other words, nature is the greatest teacher. Close your eyes and look inside. That's your core. That's the sign of your Sufism glowing, growing, sharing and loving.

Sufis and Darvishes are both without egos.

I have taught people to be Darvishes through poetry—through art, music. I break the ice through hugs. I have only been refused once, but I undid the refusal. When you insist, praise the person; the person can't keep refusing. And the wall is broken down. In relationships or friendships, once you move to evaluate, you move to judge. And no one wants to be judged. Praise, if there's reason. And if the person's unpraisable, then remain silent. Criticism puts a wall between people. Negativity feels bad. And you cannot get any friendship out of that.

If there is any pain in loving, it is one-sided. And if you love in order to receive love, you're empty. Just like going to a store wanting to buy without money. You've got to invest yourself, and that investment is the love you have in you. And the more you spend it, the stronger it becomes. Therefore, there's no loss in loving. When you are afraid of loving, no one in the world can fill the void within.

You're empty when your heart is closed. The way you fill yourself up is to open your heart. A closed heart represents inexperience, fear of not knowing. Instead it should be excitement of new things, new breath, new friends, or simply newness. You take a shower every day; you open your heart every day. Cleansing your heart. And soon after, you will never be closed.

To bring more love to people, I hug them, make them laugh, insult myself. As long as I make them laugh, it gets me closer. Ask them questions that I know they know the answer to, to give them confidence. How are you going to live your life with me in it? I also share my ailments, my shortcomings. I don't hide anything from them. No reason to be different from who you are when you're with other people. Harmony is a positive exchange. That's very important. Friendship is like music. If one person is out of tune, the whole thing falls. If I could only give one thing to a stranger in need, it would be a hug. Once we do that, we're no longer strangers.

I don't think I would be alive without love. Going through life, no matter how difficult it was, love carried me through. Love is like a wing, which always ascends you. And if you carry the problems of the day, you won't go too high and you won't crash.

In friendship, my heart is bottomless—deeper than deep. In a word, it is infinitely open. First of all, I want you to be who you are, because who you are is beautiful. And if you changed, I don't know if I would like you. Besides, if you need to change, it would be worth it. It would be your nature. Friendship without limits.

In 5 words, this is how I try to live my life:
Love life with no resistance.
Flight, Love, Hugs, Smile, Laughter

I am like the cup of wine
　　which surrenders all that I contain
　　　　with the touch of your lips

I am like that pearl
　　which belongs to anyone
　　　　who opens my heart

I am that fallen tree
　　which will warm any soul
　　　　who puts a spark in me

I am that ray of light
　　that brings the vision of love into your eyes

I am a beggar who begs to give you love

I am a Sufi

Epilogue to My Journey

I learned love from a dog. I learned friendship in the Revolution. I learned how to be a Sufi from a Sufi musician. I learned togetherness in the Revolution, where we got together at night as a group for safety. I learned communication from a cat, who came back from dying and started biting my neck where he used to. I learned the meaning of sacrifice when I lost my friends in the Revolution. I am now in peace that my own life experiences have made me realize life itself and where I fit in. All else doesn't matter. Friendship and love is all that matters.

All the above was engraved in me by the environment I grew up in. My mother was the center of it all, my father was the protector and my friends supported me. And I am indebted to them all for whom I have become. Today I am the collection of all who have loved me and taught me, fed me, sang to me, listened to my songs and put me to sleep at night, preparing me for a new day of breathing in the universe and breathing out friendship. I don't plan to live long. I plan to live one day at a time. No, let me amend that. I plan to live one breath at a time. This is my life, my story, my biography. The real biography belongs to those who brought me to this earth and some day will take me from this earth.

When the time comes, I will be buried in a nearby Whitmore Lake cemetery. Come and visit me. I will still have something to say beyond this life. Connecting hearts will not die, will not be buried. It is a forever relationship. My friends, I will not be denied loving you.

You will never find me

If a tear drops by
    or a smile brushes your face
    or a song bursts of out of your chest
You will know I have come to visit

My legacy I intend to leave is the things that I have created, the poems that I have written, the photography that I have done, the friendships that I have gathered and the hugs I have left with friends. I have never refused a hug by friends, strangers, children, trees or cats. Never refused the essence of roses. Never said 'no' to friends. When I look at someone, my eyes say 'I don't know you, but I love you. Let us be friends no matter the age, the sex, the color or religion.' And the happiness I shared among whoever comes near me, will always be with me. [Hosain's blood type is B Positive!]

If I had the opportunity, what would I change in my life? Nothing, for I have hugged trees—any, all or any endangered species—like loving humans. Changing only brings regret. Going back means repressing, contracting—the future has to go, so I can go back to something. Today, I am the collection of all my mistakes, all my successes, and I wouldn't want to change any of them. That's what I am today.

The bucket on my bucket list is full of holes. I always have a need of room for everything that comes to me. A bucket means 'containing something.' So, I don't want to contain anything. That means you have to live with old things. You need to be prepared always to receive, to understand and look forward to the next thing. In other words, anything that comes to me is in my bucket without limits. My only unfinished goal that I would like to accomplish is life. Finish life, leaving a sense of loving and brotherhood.

What is it that I have wanted to do but remains undone? What I want to do, will never be done: brotherhood of man. I am unable to reach and touch and be touched enough. You taste one drop of an ocean, you know the taste of the whole ocean. You love one person, you become a lover for the rest of your life. As for me, I don't think I can reach that far. But I keep trying.

Several times in my life, I almost died. It is coming to me that the reason I am alive today is to share what I can offer. And that is, in fact, the very reason for any human being to be alive: to spread enduring love and care and to join for the safety of humanity, so that we can stand together as beacons of love. No one is too small to rise and touch another soul. In the name of love and compassion, we stand together to mend the dignity of mankind. The integrity of mankind has been scarred, and my biography should end with that I stood up for love, no matter how many times I was struck down. The only accomplishment I want to be remembered for is that I have loved enough, that I have made more friends than enemies, and that I was there when I was needed; and I am grateful to be here. I am humbled to live among you, my dear ones. In oneness, we become one family of mankind. We can heal and be healed. We can sing, dance and be merry in any language. We need to be the eyes for those who are unable to see. We need to be the voices of people everywhere. This is our destiny. I live to see this.

So sadly, Hosain passed away March 8, 2018. His love is smiling down on all of us. As he said,

My life is a gift
My treasure is my friends
My future is infinity
My death is a bargain
I take birth every moment

When my time comes
nothing will remain
but love

Printed in the United States
By Bookmasters